COLLISION
with the
INFINITE

COLLISION
with the
INFINITE

A Life Beyond
the Personal Self

SUZANNE SEGAL

BLUE DOVE PRESS
SAN DIEGO • CALIFORNIA • 1996

Blue Dove Press publishes books by and about sages and saints of all religious and authentic spiritual traditions as well as other spiritually and inspirationally oriented works. Catalog sent free upon request. Write to:

Blue Dove Press, P. O. Box 261611, San Diego, CA 92196 telephone: (619) 271-0490

FIRST EDITION

Cover and text design:
  Brian Moucka, Poppy Graphics, Santa Barbara, California

Special thanks to Stephan Bodian for significant help in the production of this edition

Cover adapted from art by Richard Kirsten—Daiensai. Used with permission of the artist.

For sources of copyrighted materials see page 173.

ISBN: 1-884997-27-9

The names of certain people appearing in this book have been changed where deemed appropriate.

The author may be contacted at:
              Suzanne Segal
              P. O. Box 218
              Stinson Beach, CA 94970

Library of Congress Cataloging-in-Publication data:
Segal, Suzanne
    Collision with the Infinite : a life beyond the
personal self /
  Suzanne Segal. -- 1st ed.
        p. cm.
    ISBN 1-884997-27-9
    1. Spiritual life. 2. Sunyata. 3. Segal,
Suzanne
        I. Title.
BL624.S434   1996
291.4'092--dc20
[B]   96-31842
                             CIP

CONTENTS

FOREWORD

There is only one reality, one truth, one consciousness that peers out through your eyes and my
eyes right now. It is the ultimate subject of all objects,
the ground of being in which all manifestation arises
and passes away and of which all apparently objective
existence consists. As Meister Eckhart puts it, "The
eyes with which I see God are the eyes with which
God sees me." Call it Buddha nature or spirit, emptiness or Self—all religions point to it and provide various methods to approach it. Yet, as the esoteric
traditions make clear, it is an indescribable mystery
that cannot be known through the mind.

The separate self that yearns to realize the truth
must first be seen for what it is—a compelling construct with no abiding existence—before we can
awaken to the recognition that we are nothing other
than this mystery. As the great sages repeatedly
remind us, "The seeker is the sought; the looker is

what he is looking for." There is no other, just this! At this point, of course, words fail us, and we are left with awe in the face of the ungraspable.

In every era, a few rare individuals have appeared to remind us, through their unshakable conviction and clarity, that who we really are is the ungraspable itself. Because they are beyond all limited identities and do not see others as separate or endarkened in any way, such beings have characteristically declined to accept the role of teacher or guru. Ramana Maharshi, for example, the great sage of south India, received all who came to him as the one sacred and indivisible Self. This book introduces yet another who points us directly to our identity with the mystery— Suzanne Segal.

Like Ramana's, Segal's realization occurred abruptly, unexpectedly, and without preparation. One moment she was waiting for a bus, the next moment she was no one. Her personal identity as Suzanne Segal dropped away in an instant, never to return. The autobiography you hold in your hands is the extraordinary story of how a young Jewish woman from the Midwest came to terms with this powerful transformation despite the mind's relentless attempts to pathologize it, and how the experience ultimately blossomed into full Self-realization.

I first met Suzanne Segal when she appeared in my psychotherapy office in 1992 seeking help with the fear that had plagued her for 10 years. Ever since her personal identity had disappeared, her mind had been either struggling to reconstruct it (to no avail) or generating the terrifying belief that something must be horribly wrong with her. Turning to Western psychology for answers, she had even completed her doctoral training and become a clinical psychologist in an attempt to make sense of the experience. Before me, she had consulted nearly a dozen therapists, all of whom had concurred that she had a serious problem—though, of course, none of them had succeeded in curing her.

When I heard Suzanne describe her abiding state of consciousness, I knew immediately that she had experienced a profound spiritual awakening, and I told her so. What I didn't understand, however, was why she was feeling so much fear. I suggested she take her question to my teacher, Jean Klein, who happened to be visiting the area giving dialogues on advaita (non-dualism). After verifying that the absence of a "me" was far from a problem, as she had assumed, but rather the "perfect" state of being, Jean offered some succinct suggestions for how she might relate to her fear. I did not see her again for nearly three years.

In November of 1994 I received a phone call from Suzanne asking me to help her edit her spiritual autobiography. What she had written was a skeletal account of her "collision with emptiness" and the years that followed. I agreed to help her develop this kernel into a more complete account of her journey and immediately began encouraging her to fill in the details, particularly her childhood and her years of TM practice. Although she had no particular interest in talking about her personal life—after all, she no longer identified herself as a person—she took my advice when I argued that a fuller description would engage the reader and make more accessible the story of her awakening and the mind's struggle to come to terms with it. Chapter by chapter, the autobiography assumed its present form.

As we worked together, it became apparent to me that the frightened woman who had come to my office for help three years before had been transformed. The Suzanne I now encountered was a fearless, joyful being who radiated love and whose spiritual wisdom was equal to that of the Zen and advaita adepts I most respected. At the same time, I found her to be thoroughly ordinary, thoroughly accessible, and thoroughly lacking in pretense or ambition—qualities I had learned in my Zen days to recognize as hallmarks of the awakened state.

I asked Suzanne if she would be willing to trade our time, and she agreed. For every hour I worked on the book, she spent an hour helping me to clarify and refine my own spiritual understanding. In particular, I had always believed that the presence of fear—which I experienced often, and for no apparent reason— meant that, despite years of practice and numerous insights into the nature of being, I must be doing something wrong that prevented me from integrating my insights into my moment-to-moment existence. If only I could get rid of the fear, I reasoned, then I would be free. But the more I struggled with it, trying to breathe or cathart or love it away, the more seemingly solid and entrenched it became.

What Suzanne helped me to realize was that fear doesn't mean anything except that fear is present. It does not obscure our true nature unless we believe the story it tells us or take it to mean something it does not. In fact, the infinite awareness that is our true identity contains everything within it, including all mental and emotional states. Fear, anger, jealousy, sadness, and other seemingly "negative" emotions are there too, like seaweed floating in the limitless ocean of ourselves. There just doesn't happen to be a separate self to whom they refer. After all, if the infinite—which we all are intrinsically—is indeed infinite, how could it be otherwise?

After about six months, and some significant breakthroughs on my part, I began suggesting to Suzanne that I introduce her to a few of my friends. As with everything else, she said it would happen when it was "obvious," and so it was not until the waning days of 1995 that about a dozen of us met one afternoon at the home of a friend. Other gatherings followed, each one larger than the last, and within a few months several hundred people were crowding a local church to hear her tell her story and respond to questions.

Despite the growing attention, however, Suzanne refuses to refer to herself as a teacher. Instead, she insists that she is a "describer" of the "naturally occurring state" of every one of us. No matter who we think we are or how misguided we imagine ourselves to be, she reminds us, we are in reality the ground of being itself—what she calls the "vastness," the infinite substance of which everything consists and in which everything abides. This vastness does not belong to anyone in particular; in fact, there is no separate self anywhere to whom it could possibly belong.

As editor-in-chief of the magazine *Yoga Journal* for ten years, I have developed a healthy skepticism for those who take themselves to be spiritual teachers. After spending many hours with Suzanne as editor, advisor, and friend, I can say with complete confidence that this remarkable woman—neither teacher, guru, nor sage—is precisely who she describes herself to be in these pages. There is truly no one home—and in this absence the infinite is revealed.

I believe that Suzanne's unique way of expressing the timeless truths of our non-dual nature has the potential to reach many people who might not otherwise be drawn to them, and I think this little book is destined to become a spiritual classic. I am happy to have played a part in birthing it into being.

Stephan Bodian
Mill Valley, California
June 1996

INTRODUCTION

As Westerners seeking spiritual transformation, we need to help each other out by sharing our stories. Since we encounter spiritual experiences in ways that Easterners do not, we need to gather our accounts of transformation in order to create new "ancient texts" that provide Western-style maps of the spiritual territory. The stories of the ancestors described a road that has since seen new construction erected along its course. It's like that with roads. Just when we think we know them perfectly, someone comes along and builds new gas stations or traffic signals or grocery stores, and we have to orient ourselves all over again using new landmarks.

The story that follows is my contribution to the modern version of the ancient texts. It is an account of the fourteen-year aftermath of a complete and irrevocable shattering of personal identity, a permanent switching off and falling away of everything I had called my individual self. This profound transformation has been described in many of the classic spiritual texts of the East. However, because of my cultural beliefs, upbringing, values, and fears, I encountered it in a particularly Western fashion. The experience was so different from anything I had previously imagined or conceived that its impact took more than a full decade to assimilate. During that time I searched for written accounts of similar experiences that might help me through the most challenging and terrifying times of the mind's response to the totally ungraspable emptiness of "me-ness," but I found none. This book was born of the desire to provide a context and a companion for those whose destiny it is to experience the emptiness of personal self thrusting itself to the foreground in unimaginable ways.

The experience of no-self brings with it a cessation of personal history, removing forever the "person" to whom those events relate. The history remains a story only, a narrative without an author, events without personal meaning; it no longer belongs or refers to a "me."

There is a notion in the West that one must have a personal self in order to function adequately in the world—that it is the self that holds together, and exists as, all that one is. Without a self, it is believed, one would be reduced to a form of idiocy or insanity, neither of which resembles anyone's notion of awakening into truth.

As Westerners we cannot help but be terrified at the prospect of the individual self revealing itself to be empty. After all, in the West the personal self is invested with the highest value. This story's description of the state of living every moment without a personal reference point makes it clear that it is in no manner a non-functional condition. The chronicle of this "life beyond the personal self" provides a modern version of what the ancestors have described, but adds the experience of the journey itself, which they did not provide. Even if they had described their experience of the journey, it would certainly have been vastly different, since they lived in a cultural context that honored rather than devalued or pathologized their experience.

It was at the suggestion of my editor that I included the story of who "I" was before the "I" was no more. It has been a challenge to write about the person who was Suzanne Segal before the personal self fell away. The story of that life is a fiction about a character who no longer exists. The person who writes this book is one who is empty of personal identity but who retains the memory of a story that does not fit the traditional notions of what awakening is thought to look like. In fact, the realization that awakening may not correspond to traditional pictures is one of the most significant messages this life has to convey.

Do not make the mistake of reading the story of Suzanne Segal searching for the childhood events that "caused" the subsequent dropping away of self. There is no linear causality at work here. The powerful influence of Western psychology in our culture has led many to believe that the roots of all human experience lie in early childhood and that psychological theories can account for any point on the continuum. The events of our past tell us about the personal, not the impersonal; about the individual self, not the universal Self. It is essential that this story be read with a spacious awareness that eschews reductionist categorization or the psychological tendency to pathologize.

Also, please remember as you read that the formalities of language oblige one to use personal pronouns in conveying an experience that is no longer personal. The "I" that you read on the paper refers to no one, but it is impossible to tell the story without using words like "I," "me," and "mine." The mystery in which all abides is infinitely vast.

COLLISION
with the
INFINITE

1.

EARLY YEARS

Behind the world our names enclose
is the nameless.
            —*Rainer Maria Rilke*

I used to meditate on my name. As a child of seven or eight I would sit cross-legged, eyes closed, on the long white couch in my parent's living room and say my name over and over to myself. The name would reverberate in my mind with each repetition, starting off solid and strong. My name, who I was. Then fainter, repeating, repeating, repeating, until a threshold was crossed and the identity as that name broke, like a ship released suddenly from its mooring to float untethered on the ocean waves. Vastness appeared. The name became a word only, a collection of sounds pulsing in a vast emptiness. There was no person to whom that name referred, no identity as that name. No one.

Then fear would arise, my heart would pound hard in my ears, and I would struggle for air, my lungs squeezed in fear's iron grip. I would stop, get up from the couch, walk around, force myself back from the vastness and into the identity of that name. It was too frightening to bear for one so young. But later that day I would return to the couch, sit again, start the name.

I will never know what compelled me to do this practice or how the idea of it ever arose. But the dropping away of personal identity, the dissolution of I-ness that occurred in this daily practice when I was just a young child, was only a preparation, a foreshadowing, for the profound and permanent state that has become my abiding reality. The journey began when that name was peeled away, leaving a mountain of emptiness in its stead. This is where the story begins.

I was the second child and only daughter of parents who came as immigrants to this country—my father when he was just a boy of five and my mother when she was twenty-eight years old. Both my parents had suffered severe hardships throughout their lives, but my mother in particular exuded the poignant melancholy of one who had witnessed decades of human cruelty. As a Holocaust survivor, she bore a sadness so solid and deep that time has never diminished it.

My father survived his early hardships by toughening externally, a tactic that contributed to making him one of the most successful businessmen in his field. A self-made man, he emerged out of a generation of immigrants who were able, with virtually no formal education, to achieve an extraordinary level of material success. Setting out to build an empire, he succeeded in accomplishing just that. He chose a woman who matched his ideal of beauty and artistic accomplishment and proposed to my mother after he had known her for only two weeks. She had just come to this country from Italy, where she had been living after escaping from a Polish work camp during the war.

When I was four years old, I wanted desperately to learn to read. I would go to the public library with my mother and sit for hours in the children's room with one of the large, brightly colored books propped open on my knees. I would stare at the writing, those black lines on the white pages, and pour all my force of concentration onto the page, trying to break the mysterious code. I was able to make out two or three words, and each time I found them I would experience a moment of joy.

I made my mother read to me several times a day from my favorite storybooks, oversized, glossy, cartoonish volumes. Sitting in her lap watching carefully as she read, I memorized every word and knew exactly when to turn each page. I delighted in showing off to my mother's friends when they visited, excitedly "reading" the books to them in my best grown-up voice, turning the pages in just the right places. When my parents hosted a large gathering at our home, I would pull up the little stool from the kitchen and climb up to recite the stories I had memorized. There was a deep pleasure that came from being the knower of those stories, the teller of those tales. To this day, whenever I have occasion to see my parents' friends, they inevitably reminisce mistily about the times I recited stories to them while standing on the kitchen stool in my frilly party dress and patent leather shoes.

My mother's legacy was not only one of sorrow, it was also one of fear. When I was little, I was terrified every time she left the house—so terrified that I often called her just so I could hear her voice and have her tell me the exact time she and my father would be home. I would stand at the window that looked out over the driveway, staring into the night like one keeping a vigil, waiting for their return. Only when their car pulled into the driveway would I go to my bed to sleep. The fear of generations had been passed down to me through my mother, and out of my love for her I shouldered it without a second thought, hoping perhaps to relieve her of what seemed like an overwhelming burden.

During my high school years, my mother was constantly distraught about my choice of friends. She was sure I had fallen in with "the wrong crowd" who were having a bad influence on me. Although it was true that my friends at the time were the "revolutionaries," my mother never understood that I always maintained the role of observer of my friends. I watched without really participating in the counterculture of the late sixties and early seventies. I chose friends who flung themselves fearlessly into every experience that came their way, but I was too caught up in my own fear to do anything but watch.

When I was fifteen, my mother journeyed with her aunt to Italy to visit the people who had helped her when she had escaped there after the war. During this trip, she succumbed to the monster of her sorrow and fell into a deep depression that necessitated, upon her return, a ten-day stay in a psychiatric hospital. I took over as "acting mother" of the family while she was hospitalized, looking after my two brothers and my father as best I could. My mother and I switched roles at that time and never switched back again. Even after she returned, I would drive her around wherever she needed to go, help her buy clothes or groceries, and tend to the needs of the family when I got home from school.

At the same time, I was experiencing a reaction to this pattern, making my adolescence a stormy one filled with anger and despair about the future. This volatile mixture, combined with the upheaval taking place in the culture at large, catapulted me, fear and all, into a quest for either solace or escape from the sorrow that circulated inside me like the blood in my veins.

The summer I graduated, I set off for the mountains of Wyoming to participate in Outward Bound. High school had provided me with four years of turmoil, confusion, and experimentation—a fairly typical adolescent experience—and the suburban environment where I lived seemed to be closing in on me, stifling my sensibilities and crushing an inner yearning that sought an indefinable freedom. I signed up to spend six weeks in the wilderness of the Wind River Range with a group of about twenty other young people and four adult guides, hiking and camping in the high country, learning survival skills, whitewater maneuvers, and methods for walking the earth with respect.

I yearned to experience a vastness that I knew so intimately yet had never encountered in the world. I

found it in those mountains. Each night, while everyone else in the group slept, I wandered the area
around our campsite under the hugeness of the sky,
moved beyond belief at the immensity of the night. It
was in those mountains that I met silence again, never
knowing when the first time had been yet needing no
more than a moment of its presence to rejoice at our
reunion. Silence was my first love.

When I was eighteen, I started to meditate. I was
just ending my first year at Lake Forest College, a
small private school not far from my parents' home. I
had chosen to stay close by out of some unspoken yet
deeply felt agreement with my mother.

During spring break, my older brother, Dan,
told me about Transcendental Meditation. It was
1973, and TM was making quite a splash among
the college crowd. Apparently the Beatles and
Donovan had just spent time with Maharishi in
India, thus endorsing for an entire generation his
particular brand of spiritual practice. The closest
TM center to Lake Forest was located in a small
house near the campus of Northwestern University
in Evanston, just north of Chicago.

On a balmy spring evening I went to an introduc-
tory lecture at the center given by two tall, thin young
men who were dressed—incongruously for their age
and the time—in suits, ties, and wing-tip shoes. They
talked in calm, quiet voices about the benefits of
meditation, the scientific research that substantiated
their claims, and the logistics and costs of learning

how to meditate. I enrolled that evening in the next course to be offered, which began the following Saturday morning. I was told to report to the center at nine in the morning with some fresh flowers, a few pieces of fruit, and a clean, white handkerchief.

I arrived early for my appointment and was asked to fill out some forms to provide the information my teacher needed to select a mantra for me. The teacher, Ross, called me from the waiting room into a small bedroom with an altar presided over by a large, gold-framed photograph of a stern-looking Indian man sitting cross-legged on a tiger skin. My offerings of fruit, flowers, and handkerchief were placed on the altar in a small woven basket, from which Ross selected one flower, which he handed to me without a word. I stood in silence next to him, holding my flower and staring into the eyes of the stern man in the photo. Ross picked up the rest of the flowers, dipped one of them into a small brass bowl holding what appeared to be water, and began singing melodiously in Sanskrit. He never glanced in my direction, so I just watched and waited, assuming he would let me know when it was time to meditate.

Ross sang for about four or five minutes, offering the flowers, fruit, and handkerchief to the man in the photo by placing them sequentially onto a rectangular brass platter at his feet. Each offering had a chant of its own. Finally, when all the offerings were made, Ross sank to his knees in front of the altar and pressed his forehead to the floor for a moment. When he arose, he turned to me as he intoned what at first sounded like part of his Sanskrit chant, but which I soon understood to be my mantra. He gazed at me solemnly, indicating that I should repeat the mantra as he was doing, saying it aloud over and over in a normal tone of voice. He nodded his head as I repeated it and motioned me to sit down in the chair just behind me.

I kept repeating the mantra out loud until he instructed me to begin saying it more and more softly, then just silently to myself. I closed my eyes and started meditating. After a few minutes, I could feel myself settling down. Within a few more minutes, I knew I would meditate for the rest of my life. Sitting in that chair, repeating that Sanskrit word to myself in my mind, I was tenderly drawn into the embrace of my beloved silence.

⟞⟩⟩⟩⟩⟩⟩⟩⟩⟩

As my first year of college came to an end, I began to feel restless, and I knew it was time to leave my familiar suburban world. I decided to transfer to a college in Olympia, Washington, where an innovative, experimental program had just begun in an attempt to integrate the vision of the sixties into a state-sanctioned educational system. At Evergreen State College I experienced a tremendous freedom, born of living in an extraordinarily beautiful natural environment and being surrounded by like-minded souls who were giddy with the infinite possibilities that our shared idealism and youthful energy had to offer. There I met Dan, the resident TM teacher, through whose friendship I became more intimately acquainted with the astonishing mystery of the spiritual realm.

Dan became my closest friend and my first spiritual companion, sharing with me an excitement for the unexplainable, the transcendental, the indescribable. We were companions in silence, prowling the lush, fern-laden forests around the campus on our twilight walks, drinking in the intoxicating stillness. One evening, we set out for a walk quite late. The night was pitch black; even the stars were veiled by dense clouds. As we stepped into the forest, Dan extended his right arm in front of him and made a sweeping gesture from left to right. Within seconds our path was illuminated by a gossamer light that radiated out of each molecule of the air. Each plant gave off a soft glow from within itself that expanded steadily as we moved deeper into the woods. Noticing my amazement, Dan turned to me with a look of gentle warmth.

"You see, Suzanne, this light is always with us, contained in all of life. We are never in darkness, even when it appears to be night. Never forget that this world you see around you is not what it appears to be at first glance."

"Dan, how did you do that?" I asked. "You're the one who started everything glowing like this."

"No, it's not me," he said. "I'm only showing you what's present at each moment, always. We only need to attune our attention to it. I didn't create it, I'm simply pointing it out to you."

2.

THE TRANSCENDENT FIELD

Do you think I know what I'm doing?
That for one breath or half-breath I belong to myself?
As much as a pen knows what it's writing,
or the ball can guess where it's going next.
　　　　—Rumi

During Christmas break from Evergreen, I signed up for a meditation retreat at a college just down the road from Lake Forest. By this time I had been meditating for about eight months, and between the profound experiences I was having in meditation and the influence of my friend Dan, I had developed an affinity for the spiritual realm. My brother came in from college to join me for this retreat, accompanied by a friend named Rick.

During the retreat I encountered my first powerful experiences of the transcendent field, which failed to fit any previous category of description and introduced me to the soon-to-be familiar frustration of attempting to describe something that defied all my enthusiastic, well-intentioned attempts at explication.

The experience of transcending had been explained to me variously as a gap in thoughts where time seems to be suspended; a time of quietness when the mantra disappears; and the "source of thought," whatever that might mean. Never had I heard a description that matched what occurred in my delighted mind as I was gripped by a tremendous power, like a huge magnet, that pulled me into a tunnel of light at infinite speed. At the same time, the tunnel itself expanded outwards at infinite speed with a tumultuous roar that rose to an ear-splitting crescendo as the infinity exploded in light. The moment of explosion marked the crossing of a threshold. In an increment of time too small to be measured, the blaze of some invisible inferno engulfed everything, turning all phenomena inside out, exposing the underside of all creation—emptiness.

Nearly three hours after I had begun meditating the first morning of the retreat, I opened my eyes and rose from my cushion as if I were drunk, walking without the sensation of possessing a body. The world no longer looked the same; solid matter had been transformed into the luminous transparency of silence.

I told my brother and his friend what had happened, forcing my mouth to speak sounds, the words striking against each other as they tumbled from my lips, gathering meaning as they dropped together into the air. Neither Dan nor Rick knew what to say. I did look slightly stunned, they agreed. Maybe I was doing something wrong. Maybe I should speak to the teachers about it.

I took one of the retreat leaders aside and described my experience. He smiled calmly at me. My eyes couldn't quite focus on his face, and light appeared to radiate from his mouth like sunshine beaming through the boughs of trees as he parted his lips to speak. He said that Maharishi taught that nothing could hurt us when we were meditating and that any experience we encountered in meditation was a good experience. He smiled at me and said softly, "Just enjoy the bliss." When I heard the word "bliss," a cool breeze of recognition swept through me in welcome acknowledgment of the only word that could come close to describing what I was feeling—bliss. This was bliss.

My mode of perceiving had been jarred out of its ordinary pattern. It was impossible to focus separately on objects because the boundaries between them had receded into the background, supplanted by a luminosity so powerful that everything in the visual field appeared to melt together into one large radiant mass.

The retreat continued, and I followed the schedule, meditating and listening to the videotaped lectures by Maharishi as I delighted in my radically altered experience of the simplest perceptual moments—sitting in a chair, gazing around the room, speaking, smiling, breathing, thinking. The change in perception lasted several weeks before it began to fade, in almost imperceptible increments, as the world of boundaries and distinctions moved to the foreground again in my perceptual field.

The retreat marked my induction into the realm of the mysterious, catapulting me out of my adolescent ennui into the arms of bliss. To complete the picture, Rick and I fell in love. We danced in the hallways and sang off-key until dawn like restless alley cats howling at the moon. He was a delightful man—warm, talented, brilliant, full of spiritual curiosity and emotional depth, willing to love with an abandon that both frightened and excited me. For the first time I encountered the hurricane of romantic love. Our relationship was entwined in the tendrils of our meditation practice, cementing our bond as partners in both the world and the spirit.

The decision to become meditation teachers was an obvious one for both of us. What else could we do? We planned to finish the academic year and then take a year off to attend the six-month teacher training course that would be offered in August. My brother was equally drawn to further his involvement with TM, so in August of 1974, Rick, Dan, and I, along with about one hundred other bright-eyed American meditators, traveled to the mountains of northern Italy to train as teachers of Transcendental Meditation.

The TM organization had leased vacation hotels in the lovely alpine village of Livigino, Italy, where we were provided with every comfort to support us in learning the "Holy Tradition." We were instructed to practice about five hours in the morning and five hours in the afternoon in a sequence of meditation, yoga asanas, and pranayama called "rounding." We were expected to do about ten to twelve "rounds" each day, each one taking about an hour to complete.

We were strongly cautioned against making any major decisions during the course because the effects of intensive meditation would cause us to "unstress," a condition we came to both fear and joke about incessantly. Maharishi was scheduled to visit us on several occasions; as it turned out, however, we only saw him once, at the end of the training, when he arrived to initiate us as teachers and pass on the mantras that we would then use to initiate our students.

The training in Maharishi's tradition was a rigorous one. He demanded we memorize everything word for word, in phrasing that more closely approximated an Indian speaking English than any traditional American manner of speech. "It is good? It is easy?" Maharishi wanted no creative license taken with his teachings, nothing that would dilute their purity. As a result, we respectfully read over and over the wording he had chosen for every aspect of the teaching, checking and verifying our prospective students' meditations until the words echoed in our dreams.

The long hours of meditation wreaked havoc with some people's memories, but we were for the most part a young and resilient group capable of withstanding the multileveled assault on our mental faculties. There were a few, however, who were unable to tolerate the intensity, and I witnessed several painful encounters between these individuals and the course leaders, who had determined that anyone who was exhibiting too many symptoms of unstressing would be considered an inappropriate candidate to complete teacher training and be dismissed from the course.

One woman who began to hear the "voices of the angels" was moved to a room next to the course leader's and told to begin cutting down her meditation until she was sitting only twenty minutes a day. Then she was asked to leave the course. She became furious and demanded to speak with Maharishi privately about the decision. Her request was denied, and a guard was posted at her door to prevent her from leaving her room or speaking with anyone from the course. Screams, shouts, and hysterical crying could be heard emanating from her room, but we never saw her again. Our only information was provided by the course leader, who maintained that she was fine and that one of her family members had come to collect her.

At the end of the course, just before Maharishi arrived, one young man began exhibiting severe paranoia. He haunted the hallways of the hotel, springing from doorways to rant about communist plots, spy telescopes trained on his window, and bugging devices in his room. He tried to intercept Maharishi as he entered the hotel to warn him of the dangers lurking inside, but Maharishi merely smiled at him and offered him a pink rose while signaling the course leader to prevent him from approaching any further. Arrangements were soon made for the young man's departure. Frankly, we all worried about him and secretly prayed that nothing like that would happen to us.

In retrospect, it seems extraordinary that more of us didn't become "troublesome," given the many hours of meditation we were doing, exposing ourselves to large doses of what was clearly a powerful practice. We never talked much among ourselves about our own unstressing because we all seemed to have developed an intuitive fearfulness about being overheard, taken out of context, or reported to the course leaders. The realization eventually dawned on us that an atmosphere of mistrust was brewing around us and edging ever closer, even though no one allowed themselves to admit the seriousness of the situation.

For myself, I tried not to think too deeply about what was going on. I was excited and inspired by what I was learning, and I felt honored to be taking my place in the Holy Tradition as I assimilated the wisdom of the ancients. All this, and I was only twenty years old! As long as I pushed aside my concerns about the movement, I felt I was living as close to perfection as I ever imagined possible.

The experiences I encountered in meditation during those months of "rounding" were a mixture of awe-inspiring and terrifying, as I became more acquainted with the hot breath of fear as it scorched my insides and rattled my bones. Bliss had forsaken me. As soon as I closed my eyes to meditate, a great vastness would appear. The sensation of being pulled across a threshold into the infinite came more and more quickly, and I began to meditate cautiously, trying to hold myself back, fearing the moment of stepping into the emptiness of the transcendent field. I was afraid that I would never come back and that someone would find my body sitting on the bed days later, empty. "If I could only take someone with me," I thought to myself, "then it wouldn't be so scary."

I found it hard to believe that this was really a normal part of meditation, and the intensity of the experience made me worry that I might be in some kind of danger. I resolved to ask Maharishi about it, but I didn't get to pose the question for another year, during which time the fear grew, taking up residence in my guts like some uncontrollable parasite. As far as I knew, I was the only one wrestling with fear or having such experiences, which only increased my distress.

Maharishi had told us that if we meditated for six to eight years we would definitely get enlightened. He had given us specific, detailed descriptions of the states we would encounter as signposts of awakening—signposts that consciousness was being liberated into the Oneness of Unity Consciousness. Enlightenment, he said, came about in three distinct stages. The first was Cosmic Consciousness, the stage characterized by the witness, an awareness that watched while remaining separate from all phenomena and that was not overshadowed by the cycles of waking, dreaming, or sleeping. The witness, in other words, remained "awake" even as the body and mind slept, dreamed, or functioned in the world.

The next stage was God Consciousness, in which one perceived the manifest world as resplendent with sacredness, even though a separation continued to exist between "I" and "other." In this stage, the witness, which had previously remained detached and flat, disappeared in "God's consciousness," which was a sublime realm of perception permeated with divine love.

The final stage was Unity Consciousness, in which separation of any kind was obliterated as consciousness expanded to encompass all of creation. The Unity state did not admit any duality, was bathed in the purity of Oneness, and was final and complete. Maharishi always told us that Unity could not be reached without a guru because we were incapable of identifying it when it arrived. Only the guru could recognize it and, in that recognition, transmit a finality to the disciple by saying, "Yes, that's it!"

I was glad that Maharishi would recognize Unity Consciousness, because that left me free from any worry about trying to figure it out myself. With these explanations of enlightenment, which seemed so clear and complete at the time, I entrusted myself to the ocean of transcendental awareness, letting my concerns float in its waters, lulled by the promise that I would wash up on the shores of Unity Consciousness before too long.

***

After completing teacher training, Rick, Dan, and I returned to the Midwest. We were charged with enthusiasm and began teaching immediately at the center in Evanston where I had first started meditating two years before. It was an exciting time to be involved with the TM organization, as hundreds of people came each month to learn the practice. We were kept busy lecturing, initiating, and running the center. Rick and I taught together as much as we could, and we soon began to hatch plans to start a new TM center in Highland Park, Rick's home town, about thirty minutes north of Evanston. We persuaded a seasoned teacher, Anne, to join us, and between her experienced guidance and our energy and fervor the center was born.

The months passed quickly, and the new center was a resounding success. My parents learned to meditate, and I recruited my father to give a lecture with me to a group of business people in the community, which was very well received. I think my parents were pleased at the influence the TM group was having on my brother and me, especially when they saw where we had been headed before we started to meditate. They were particularly relieved to know that we were now categorically opposed to using alcohol or drugs of any kind, which Maharishi had called "poisons to the nervous system," because we did not want anything to interfere with the clarity of our meditations. My parents held several gatherings at their home where Dan and I gave talks about TM and ended up initiating many of their friends and neighbors.

There were countless stories circulating at the time about the powerful positive impact TM was having on people's lives. Each one served to renew and inspire me to trust in the power of the teaching. The only time doubts still arose was when I observed the TM organization itself. Difficult though it was to acknowledge, it was obvious to me that many of the long-time teachers, especially those in positions of power and authority in the organization, were not living the message they taught. They did not radiate the qualities I had been taught to expect in experienced meditators—kindness, patience, warmth, compassion. In fact, I found many of them to be just the opposite—curt, angry, controlling, and vindictive. I managed to sustain my idealism, however, by avoiding contact with these higher authorities.

In 1976, I began hearing rumors about a new course that Maharishi would be offering the following September. Although they varied widely, the most persistent rumor suggested that he was going to start teaching us how to acquire supernormal powers. Needless to say, everyone in the organization considered this the course of the century to attend. Yet, hearing about these *siddhis* (as the powers were called in Sanskrit), I felt a deep uneasiness. I had been accustomed to hearing Maharishi answer questions about acquiring powers by responding: "It's not necessary. It's only a distraction from the real goal, which is the transcendent field." Now he was encouraging us to develop siddhis in order to "play in the finer levels of creation." My confusion and doubts deepened, but I signed up for the course anyway.

Before embarking on the six-month siddhi course, I attended a one-month advanced training, which was held in the spring of 1976 in a small ski village in France. This was the first training at which Maharishi insisted that men and women be housed separately in order to promote "one-pointedness" in our efforts to attain enlightenment. Although TM was marketed as a technique to improve everything from blood pressure to sex, those of us who attended the advanced courses knew that we were after only one thing—enlightenment. We were committed, each in our own way, to finding that elusive yet utterly fulfilling experience of Unity Consciousness, and we proceeded on faith that we would get it if we did everything Maharishi instructed us to do.

One month before we were scheduled to leave for the siddhis course in Europe, Rick proposed to me. He said he knew it was the right thing to do because we were obviously made for each other, and he just couldn't wait until we got back. I accepted immediately, thrilled that I had found a life partner who shared so many of my passions. He had already sent a letter to my parents telling them of his "intentions" and asking for their blessings. He had even purchased a beautiful diamond ring for me, which he slipped onto my finger before we went off to make the announcement to our families. They were overjoyed about our plans to wed, and we hastily arranged a celebration two weeks before our departure. We knew we would be apart for six months, since all courses by then separated men and women, but our happiness at the vow we had made to each other to spend our lives together made even the thought of such a long separation tolerable.

Hundreds of teachers from around the world were planning the attend the "six-month course," and dozens of hotels in various towns high in the Swiss Alps had been recruited to house them. I spent the first three months in Brunnen, a lovely village on the banks of Lake Lucerne. I meditated with passion, never able to get enough of it, and my experiences of transcending became clearer and clearer, even though the fear continued to arise with alarming regularity.

Each day we were asked to fill out forms describing our experiences and rating the clarity of transcendence. We were also informed that a group leader would be chosen from among us who would be responsible for gathering up the experience forms each week and reading them to one of Maharishi's representatives over the phone. This leader would also talk to headquarters daily and report all business messages to the group. I was informed that I had been chosen to be the group leader. I didn't know exactly how to react to this news, but the decision appeared to be irrevocable, so I nodded my acceptance and hoped for the best.

Rick and I wrote to each other almost every day. Like me, he was an enthusiastic meditator, and he often described the ecstatic states he had encountered, peppering his letters with passionate declarations of his love for and gratitude to Maharishi. More than once he wrote that he could now understand those who renounced the world to live the spiritual life with their guru. I wasn't quite sure what was going on in his heart, but I resolved not to worry. I knew from my own experience that the waves of emotion during long rounding were constantly changing, and it was not unusual for any of us to entertain the notion— which we idealized—of leading the life of the renunciate seeker who left the world of *maya* and lived only to achieve enlightenment. We had already heard of those who had studied with Maharishi for years, living near him wherever he was, never returning to their previous lives in the world. Said to be "married to their asana mats," these men and women were regarded with a mixture of jealousy and awe.

Maharishi was living in Hertenstein at the time, on the top floor of a hotel that housed all his long-time female devotees (definitely in the "married to their asana mats" category) and many from the upper echelon of the TM organization. He sent out word that the group leaders from each of the women's hotels would be brought to Hertenstein to join the course there. In exchange, one woman from Hertenstein would go to each of the hotels to initiate everyone in the siddhis. I was instructed to pack my bags and wait in the lobby of my hotel in Brunnen for a van to pick me up. I was ecstatic. I was going to live in Maharishi's hotel and would be among the first to receive the siddhi techniques.

Hours later the van finally arrived, already nearly filled with other women who had been gathered from the various hotels scattered among the small villages surrounding the lake. After a cold and bumpy ride through the alpine night, we approached a gingerbread house that was perched on the side of a hill commanding a grand view of the lake and surrounding mountains. As we pulled up, three women wearing white saris stepped out of the door to greet us. We were given our room assignments and then left to fend for ourselves.

My room was spacious and comfortable, providing a lovely view of Lake Lucerne and the twinkling lights of the villages that formed a necklace around it. I dropped my bags on the floor and collapsed onto the bed, falling into a deep sleep that lasted until dawn. When I awoke the next morning, I showered and began my morning rounding, anxious to see if I felt a difference meditating in Maharishi's hotel, which was rumored to be the optimum place for transcending.

After rushing through my asanas and pranayama, I closed my eyes to begin my mantra. As soon as I started repeating it, I felt like I was being sucked into a tornado. A ferocious force began whirling me around with a velocity that seemed impossible to sustain for more than a few seconds without being ripped to shreds. I tried to pry my eyes open but couldn't even find my eyes. All sensation of having a body had gone, but still the whirling continued. A split-second later it abruptly abated, and all was silence. I lay down on the bed to gather my strength, knowing that now I simply had to have Maharishi's counsel about what in the world was happening to me in my meditations. I prayed that I would be able to speak with him soon.

⟞⟝

Our arrival in Hertenstein marked the beginning of a major change in the tone of the course. We were scheduled to be initiated into the siddhis the following day by two senior devotees. Then we were supposed to begin doing the practices as a group in the downstairs banquet room, which had been converted into a meditation space. Large foam mats were laid side by side on the floor, covered by dozens of white sheets. The windows too were covered by foam mats and sheets to insure complete privacy and—as I was to learn later—to keep the noise of the siddhi-practicing women from raising suspicions with our Swiss neighbors. The room looked like an enormous padded cell, with the stately crystal chandeliers lending an air of elegant absurdity. I was not the only newcomer to burst out laughing the first time she entered the room. This strange scene seemed to confirm the rumors we had heard that we would be learning to "fly." There was simply no other explanation for the padded room except as a "landing pad" for budding fliers.

We had yet to catch a glimpse of Maharishi, though rumor had it that he would be initiating us. We were told to sit in a circle in the "foam room" and wait for instructions. As we took our places, we naturally formed into two distinct groups, the newly arrived looking slightly embarrassed and the old timers adopting an air of detached superiority. We were ready. Barbara, our course leader and a long-time devotee of Maharishi, entered the room carrying a telephone, which she placed in the center of the circle. She said that Maharishi would give us the first five siddhis by phone after we completed a *puja* (devotional ceremony) together. We were shocked. Maharishi was upstairs, but he was going to speak to us by phone?

Barbara began setting up the puja table while some women fetched flowers and fruit from the kitchen. When they returned, we all stood together, each of us holding a flower, and sang the puja in a chorus of voices. The ceremony quieted my agitated mind, and I felt an easiness return to my spirit. We bowed together at the close of the puja and formed a circle around the phone. It crackled twice, then Maharishi's high-pitched voice came through the lines sounding as if he were thousands of miles away.

"How are you, ladies?" he chimed. "Is everyone happy? Feeling relaxed?"

"We're very happy, Maharishi," Barbara replied. "There are thirty-two ladies here, and we have just finished puja."

"Very good, very good. Now we will start the process of making you all Governors of the Age of Enlightenment. You will be learning to play in the finest levels of thought now that you have gained so much from your years of meditation. All of you have been experiencing clear transcending, yes? Very good. Now your clear transcending will be put to use to bring peace to everyone on the planet. We are heralding in the Age of Enlightenment through the effects of your hours of deep meditation. Soon the whole world will be enjoying the peace and bliss that our meditation is sending out like waves to everyone."

After describing the siddhis in some detail, he gave us the exact techniques, called *sutras*, for five of the siddhis. One of them was the flying sutra. We wrote everything down as he spoke, and he told us we would be allowed to refer to our papers until we had memorized them completely. He also instructed us to meditate in our rooms for three hours in the morning and then convene downstairs in the hall to do our siddhi practice together.

The next morning, the newcomers arrived on time for our first group siddhi practice. As I sat cross-legged on the foam mat to begin the sutras, I heard the most bizarre sounds coming from around the room. My eyes flew open, and I saw that all the old-timers, who had already been practicing the siddhis for about three weeks, were swaying from side to side or back to front and letting out the most disturbing sounds I had ever heard. There were screams, yells, whispers, growls, grunts, shrieks, laughter, yelps, and groans. The room was alive with movement and sound. The rest of us were staring at each other in amazement, trying to gauge the seriousness of the event.

Our amazement quickly turned to hilarity when we witnessed the old-timers take off. "Flying" wasn't really the right word for what they were doing; it bore a closer resemblance to hopping. But there they were, sitting in lotus position with their eyes closed, letting out sounds ranging from war whoops to giggles, hopping around on the foam mats looking like frogs plopping from one lily pad to another. What a sight!

I wrote to Rick about everything that was happening in Hertenstein. His group had also been initiated

into the five beginning sutras, and he was having similar experiences, cacophony and all. Unlike me, however, he responded to the siddhis with pure delight.
He found the sutras to be exciting beyond his wildest
dreams, and he seemed to be riding a wave of happiness that knew no bounds.

The course was now in its second month in
Hertenstein, but we had yet to even catch a glimpse
of Maharishi. We kept hearing that he was doing this
or that from his suite in the hotel, and we received
letters from friends at other hotels saying how envious they were that we were right there in the center
of the action. We wrote back assuring them they had
no reason to be envious.

Because of the steady influx of devotees from
Seelisberg, those of us who were housed in Hertenstein were occasionally told to vacate our room to
make space for a newcomer. My friend Ann, who
had been with me in Brunnen, was asked to give up
her place and move to a tiny room with no bath-
room. (She would have to use the one down in the
lobby.) It happened to be Ann's birthday, and we
had decorated her door with cards and notes. She
asked to be allowed to wait until the next morning
to move so she could enjoy her birthday there. The
answer was a resounding no, said so forcefully that
Ann burst into tears.

As she stood there crying, several of the leaders
stormed into her room and began tossing her things
into the hallway. Several other course members and

I began yelling at them to stop, and a shouting match ensued. Barbara screamed that it was Maharishi's wishes they were carrying out—this was the excuse that was used for every incomprehensible request—and that it was "for your evolution" to do as Maharishi said.

Although incidents like this did not occur regularly, they arose with more frequency than one might expect from people who were practising techniques that were supposed develop higher consciousness. I found it more and more difficult to ignore the obvious lack of compassion shown by those of the inner circle, and this in turn raised long-suppressed doubts about the entire message of the organization.

Two weeks before the end of the course, there was excitement in the air as we began preparations for our "graduation" ceremony, which would take place in Seelisberg. There we would all be receiving diplomas that would certify us as Governors of the Age of Enlightenment. Maharishi had requested that the women wear saris, and those of us who had never done so before began worrying about our ability to pull it off without looking like absolute fools. An Indian woman in the course promised to give us a demonstration of how to wrap ourselves up and walk with as much grace as possible—or at least to just walk.

We still had not seen Maharishi, although he had spoken to us by phone three more times in the past month to give us additional sutras. With the new siddhis practices, meditation, hatha yoga, and pranayama, we were now spending a total of three hours to complete one round. I wondered whether it would be possible to maintain such a rigorous schedule when we got back to the States. After all, doing only one round in the morning and one in the afternoon, which was the suggested practice for life "in the world," took nearly six hours. We were also instructed to send a progress report each month to headquarters in Seelisberg describing our experiences of the siddhis.

It was a lovely, warm winter day. I had just finished lunch and was on my way out to take my daily walk in the surrounding hills when I stopped at the front desk to check my mail. There was a letter from Rick, which I snatched up and tore open eagerly. I read the first three sentences, and my heart began to pound so hard that I had to sit down to steady myself. I read the lines again. He said he didn't want to get married. He had already written to our parents, and now he was writing to me. He said he knew I would be hurt, but he had decided he couldn't marry—ever. He wanted to dedicate his life to his guru, living as near to Maharishi as possible, remaining celibate and attaining enlightenment.

I had to gasp for air as I read. I was speechless. Several friends gathered around me as I choked out the news to them with tears streaming down my face, gulping between words and finally dissolving into sobs. I cried for days, looking through the piles of letters I had received from him, trying to trace the reason for this unbearable decision. Then anger arose, stormy and strong, piecing my heart back together in its fury. I took off my diamond ring, addressed an envelope to Rick, put a stamp on it, dropped the ring into the envelope, and pushed it into the mailbox. I knew this would upset him, but I was too hurt to care. We would be seeing each other in just a week at the graduation ceremony and then flying back to the United States together. I wanted him to tell me to my face that this was what he wanted.

Early on the final morning of the course, we left for Seelisberg. Our flight was scheduled to depart from Zurich at seven in the evening, and we thought we had plenty of time to spend at the ceremony. As usual, however, organizational problems led to delays, and by the time we arrived we had about twenty minutes to receive our diplomas before leaving for the airport. I saw Rick briefly as we got off the bus. He appeared to be completely calm, almost detached. No emotion played across his face as he said hello and commented on how nice I looked in my sari. The plane ride was no better. Rick was in high spirits for the entire journey home. He seemed to be experiencing no pain whatsoever, except, as I had predicted, some anger at me for sending the ring back to him in such an irresponsible manner.

Our arrival in Chicago was met with mixed emotions by our parents. They turned out at O'Hare Airport bearing bouquets of flowers and joyous smiles that seemed to freeze in place as their gaze fell on me. The pain was evident in their eyes and in the embraces with which they greeted me, though I appreciated their efforts at joviality. None of them knew quite what to say as we walked down the long corridor to collect our baggage. Rick and I were both stunned into silence by the busyness of the world, and our families chatted perfunctorily about all the foods we must have missed while we were away and the restaurants we might like to go to for dinner.

As Rick left with his family after gathering his bags, his mother gave me a long, searching look filled with apologies that were not hers to give. My mother burst into tears when they disappeared out of sight, turning the moment into an effort to console and calm her. For once, I was genuinely happy for the diversion she provided, and I patted her back and reassured her it would all work out for the best.

After being home for barely two days, I decided to return to Switzerland for another three months. The option had always been available, and many of the women in Hertenstein had stayed on. My parents readily assented, probably hoping that another trip to Europe would heal my broken heart. I called Switzerland to make the necessary arrangements, and two days later I was on a SwissAir flight back to Zurich. I spent the next three months in Arosa, where I was finally able to ask Maharishi my question about fear when he came to see us at the end of our course.

"Maharishi," I began, "I must ask you about an experience that I've been bothered with for over a year. Whenever I have clear experiences of transcending, I'm attacked by an overwhelming fear that makes me feel like I'm going to die right there if I don't stop meditating."

Maharishi broke into peals of laughter, a response I had not anticipated.

"Don't worry about the fear," he said, still laughing. "It's just the body holding on to the world. You must let go of the world to transcend, but the body becomes afraid because it thinks the world is all there is. You must not listen to the fear of the body—just let go."

I finally had my answer, although just letting go seemed too terrifying to be an appealing alternative. Maharishi's suggestion made sense theoretically, but it would be many years—after experiences of fear infinitely more excruciating than any I had previously encountered—before letting go would finally just happen out of sheer exhaustion.

The three-month course was a continuation of the course in Hertenstein, only much bigger. The hotel Pratjali in Arosa was filled to capacity with a hundred and eighty women siddhas, as we were called, who had arrived there from various locations around Europe where they had just completed a six-month course. The grand ballroom had been turned into a cavernous siddhi arena, which echoed with the screams and yelps of the group and sent them reverberating throughout the entire hotel. We spent about six hours a day in our rooms doing rounds and another three hours in the large group doing siddhis. The cacophony was ear-splitting.

I longed for my earlier experiences of deep silence and peace, which had catapulted me into my involvement with the TM movement in the days when transcendental awareness was the sole pursuit. The siddhi courses were starting to take their toll on my peace of mind, making me feel agitated rather than blissful.

At the end of the course, I couldn't wait to leave Arosa, never to return to the madhouse that the TM organization had become. I wanted to flee from the prison of the conceptual framework I had adopted in the confines of Maharishi's world, flee and not look back, hoping the next chapter would bring what I truly sought.

3.

PRELUDE TO EMPTINESS

In the long journey out of the self
There are many detours, washed-out,
interrupted raw places
Where the shale slides dangerously
And the back wheels hang almost over the edge
At the sudden veering, the moment of turning.
                                    —*Theodore Roethke*

Once I had returned to the United States, California seemed like the obvious destination. I packed my belongings and bade my parents goodbye. I was becoming familiar with the experience of moving on in life, not by analyzing options and weighing pros and cons, but by simply stepping into the next moment and doing what was there to do. I never analyzed motivations or accumulated arguments in support of one line of action over another. I had realized early that I could trust completely that the next thing to do would make itself known in an obvious manner. The move to California was simply the next thing to do.

I registered at Sonoma State College for the fall quarter and threw myself into the academic life with a previously unknown fierceness, born surely of the loneliness of life outside a close spiritual community, mixed with an unbridled pleasure in acquiring ideas to add to the spiritual knowledge I had been steeped in. I tried not to look back, hoping that I had learned all there was to learn from my previous experiences and that nothing would come back to haunt me. For the most part I lived without memories of the past, except for the meditation experiences that continued to dance me into the field of infinite space every time I sat and closed my eyes. I meditated only sporadically after I returned from the siddhis course, finding it difficult to make time to sit quietly in the midst of such an active existence.

After years of cloistered living, I explored the life of a free, single woman with enthusiasm and joy. I drowned the pain of losing my first love in an ocean of new relationships, reveling in the excitement of exploring intimate territory with a series of different partners, each one opening me to yet another aspect of the seemingly endless prism of human beingness.

I also found inspiration in my studies. In January 1978 I transferred to the University of California at Berkeley, where I launched into a period of intensive exploration that imprinted me with a love for the human story as I worked my way through the great world literature of the nineteenth and twentieth centuries. In December 1979 I graduated with a degree in English literature and immediately began looking for the next thing to do. I didn't have to wait long; as usual, the next thing to do was waiting right there, in the next moment. I booked a flight to Paris, France.

I wish I could provide a deeper explanation for why I chose Paris. I'm sure there were many unseen influences that moved me in that direction. At the time, however, I could only say that it was the next obvious thing to do. I had studied French in high school and felt an extraordinary ease with the language, as if I were remembering it rather than learning it for the first time. Once I arrived in Paris, I found that I had a familiarity with the city itself, as if I had lived there before and already known its winding streets and vibrant energy.

I found an apartment almost immediately on the Left Bank in the St. Germain-des-Pres, one of the most colorful and lively neighborhoods of the city. I enrolled at the Sorbonne in their program for foreign students and immersed myself in a new and exciting life. I virtually inhaled the city, taking it into myself with a force that could have been experienced, had I been more inclined toward caution, as frightening. But caution was not my companion at the time, and I simply reveled in the extraordinary perfection of it all. Paris was alive in a way I had never experienced a city to be, and I felt at home in its energy, thrilled by its magic. I would wander the cobblestone streets at dawn and feel overcome with joyful wonder, finding it hard to believe I was really seeing the sights before my eyes.

My one friend in Paris was Juliette, the sister of a man I had met while attending the TM teacher training course. Juliette was a whimsical, dreamy woman who was willing to set off on any adventure at a moment's notice. We spent a great deal of time together in my first weeks in Paris, and I owe her a debt of gratitude for introducing me to the complex world of Parisian life.

It was at Juliette's apartment that I first caught sight of the philosopher Bernard-Henri Levi as he was being interviewed by a well-known journalist on a televised news program. Levi was the leader of a new movement that was deconstructing the traditional philosophical position of the twentieth century. I couldn't understand a word he was saying, but I was intrigued by his passionate manner. Juliette told me that Levi would be appearing at a rally the next day to be held in Ivry, a small suburb just south of Paris. We made plans to attend together.

I arrived in Ivry before Juliette amidst a crowd of people gathering to hear Levi speak. The rally was held in a large tent that had been set up for the occasion with dozens of rows of folding chairs facing a raised wooden platform that held a podium and several comfortable armchairs. I scanned the crowded tent for two available seats, hoping that Juliette would be able to find me if I held a place for her. I located two seats close to the center aisle about ten rows back from the front and sat down to wait. Every few moments someone would come by and ask if the seat next to me was taken. The tent was filling up quickly, and I couldn't see Juliette anywhere. Levi walked up the stairs to the stage and sat down in one of the chairs. The lights dimmed slightly, and those who weren't yet seated began the final search for an available space. A pleasant-looking man in his late twenties asked me if the seat next to me was taken. I took one more hasty look around the crowd to see if I could catch sight of Juliette and then agreed to allow him to sit next to me.

He started up a conversation immediately. Hearing my accent but unable to place it, he asked me where I was from. When he found out I was American, he seemed delighted and launched into a description of his most recent trip to the United States, which had included a circuit around California and Nevada that he breathlessly told me was one of the high points of his life. I couldn't help but be swept into his enthusiastic glow. People were now motioning us to be quiet as Levi stood at the podium ready to begin his talk. The man beside me introduced himself as Claude Cohen, shook my hand politely, and asked me if we could continue our conversation when the talk was over. I consented happily, thinking that at the very least I would get some good practice speaking French with this passionate conversationalist.

Claude and I walked to a cafe after the talk, weaving through the crowds of people who were thronging the streets. I had given up hope of finding Juliette. We spent the next several hours talking and drinking coffee, excitedly providing each other with as much information about ourselves as we could.

We laughed at the differences between our two cultures and poked fun at the typical American and French points of view. I found out that he had recently completed his studies in medicine and now worked as a doctor in private practice. He came from a Jewish family that had been forced to resettle in Paris in 1967 when they were driven out of their homeland in Tunisia, a traumatic time in his life that he described to me in minute detail.

Claude could talk about anything with a passion I had never encountered in anyone before. He was highly informed about an impressive range of topics that he had clearly spent a great deal of time discussing and thinking through—everything from the weather to the implications of the rise to power of the Mitterand Socialists. I struggled to understand everything he was saying and signaled him often to speak more slowly or to repeat what he was saying in a more comprehensible way.

When we finally took leave of each other, I knew I had met the person who would teach me to speak French like a native. We exchanged phone numbers and made plans to get together again in a few days for dinner and perhaps a movie. After that first date, Claude and I started spending all of our time together. I was delighted by the pleasure he took in every aspect of life, from the smallest details of a meal or the way the clouds looked in the sky to the most far-reaching philosophical or political theories. He seemed to possess an infinite reservoir of enthusiasm.

It soon became clear that our relationship was serious, especially when he moved himself into my apartment after our fourth date so we could spend more time together. I didn't resist his decisiveness, since I found myself charmed by his energetic and passionate manner. But what really cemented my bond with him was his family. They were just as expansive and boisterous as he, generating a warmth that washed over me and swept me into their fold with a natural love I never doubted. It was the experience of my life to attend Friday night dinners with them—his parents, his two sisters with their husbands, his brother, and any other family members who happened to drop by. Everyone talked at once in an onslaught of voices and questions, and they did everything in their power to make me feel comfortable in their midst.

—————

In November 1980, eight months after we had met, Claude and I married. The two-month bureaucratic nightmare of providing all the paperwork the French authorities demanded forced us to arrange a wedding date in late autumn, much to the chagrin of my family, who would be traveling to Paris for the first time and were not thrilled to make their maiden voyage under icy-cold, rainswept skies. My father could not come to the wedding because he had been stricken two years before with Alzheimer's disease, which was rapidly transforming him into a shadow of the man he had been. His mind was quickly disintegrating in a tragic decline we could only witness with horror, powerless to stop it.

After the thrill of the first months of married life began to wear off, I tried to settle into my new life as a Parisian wife. I had stopped meditating completely shortly after arriving in Paris, justifying the decision to myself by saying that I would just start again at some later date, no big deal. But a year had gone by, and I found that I was reluctant to resume meditating because I feared that Claude—and, I imagined, all Parisians—would disapprove. I was also angry at Maharishi, deeply disappointed in the spiritual world he represented, hurt that I hadn't found the enlightenment he had promised I would attain in six to eight years. Maybe it was the death of my own naiveté I was mourning as I lashed out at Maharishi in my mind. Maybe it was simply fear that I couldn't trust a deeper world. Whatever the justification, I embraced the "cult of surfaces" that was Parisian life.

I also found that speaking French all the time was having a remarkably distressing effect on me. Although I was able to converse with almost perfect fluency and had no trouble making myself understood, I never experienced the relief of fully communicating what I wanted to say. When we communicate with others, we relieve ourselves of our message, even if the other person doesn't completely understand it. But the messages I wanted to relieve myself of didn't seem to be carried by the French language; it was like making sounds that had no meaning to me. As a result, I walked around carrying a weight of uncommunicated messages that were doomed never to be sent, not because of any flaw in those who would receive them, but because the medium available to me had little connection to what was going on inside me.

I began to feel trapped. The happiness I had enjoyed during the years of regular spiritual practice had dimmed to a faint memory. A crust of despair and cynicism had formed around me, making it impossible to deny that I had been gripped by a deep loneliness. The loneliness soon gave way to intense anxiety and then began erupting with alarming frequency into full-blown panic attacks. I was sinking into confusion while desperately trying to look like I had everything under control.

Around this time, Claude started to talk about having a child. Although this came as absolutely no surprise to me, it did not immediately strike me as a wonderful idea. I had known from the moment I had met Claude's family that to marry him was to consent to having children—as many and as soon as possible. This did have its appeal, of course, especially in such a large, boisterous, warm-hearted clan. But the prospect of having a child while in the throes of a profound internal crisis made me balk for some time.

Unwilling to tell Claude the truth about my dilemma, I told him I wanted us to explore more of the world before settling down to parenthood. He agreed reluctantly, aware by this time that he had married a woman he found it hard to comprehend who might be trying to change the rules he had assumed I had understood and willingly agreed to when we wed. What he didn't realize was that I would never have concocted a specific plan with the sole intent of foiling his desires. I simply knew that the next thing to do right then was not to have a child, but to travel. The time for the child would come soon enough.

Nineteen eighty-one was our traveling year. We roamed Morocco, Italy, Amsterdam, and the South of France, spending long, lazy days in the quaint villages of the countryside where I found a timelessness that smoothed the frayed edges of my sense of entrapment. I felt freer when I was out of Paris, and my heart felt quieter, touched by the silence of nature's exquisite palette as revealed in the endless variety of her landscapes. I began to remember joy.

On our return from Sicily in January 1982, I announced to Claude that I was ready to have a child. Within a few weeks, in mid-February, I became pregnant and was immediately swept into the nauseous timelessness of baby-growing. Nurtured on cultural fantasies of radiant mothers-to-be, I was ill prepared for the physical challenges of pregnancy. The nausea and fatigue that settled in from the first week marked the beginning of the end of my experience of personal history. After those first months of pregnancy, nothing would ever be the same again, as I hurtled toward a collision with a force so mysterious and unnamable that no one could ever have prepared me for its impact.

4.

COLLISION WITH EMPTINESS

Praise to the emptiness that blanks out existence.
Existence:
This place made from our love for that emptiness!
Yet somehow comes emptiness,
    this existence goes.
Praise to that happening, over and over!
For years I pulled my own existence out of emptiness.
Then one swoop, one swing of the arm,
    that work is over.
Free of who I was, free of presence, free of
    dangerous fear, hope,
    free of mountainous wanting.
The here-and-now mountain is a tiny piece of a
    piece of straw
    blown off into emptiness.
                        —Rumi

Life proved increasingly challenging as the first months of my pregnancy progressed. In retrospect, I can see that the radical shift of reality that was about to occur began to make itself known from the day I became aware of having conceived.

Shortly after verifying that I was indeed pregnant, Claude and I drove the twenty miles to his parents' apartment to break the news of their impending grandparenthood. As we made our way along the congested highway, I noticed a perplexing sensation. My body seemed to be dissolving, losing its solidity and disintegrating into the air around me. As I looked out through my eyes, I actually perceived my body's form transmuting as it became infused with a spacious, foggy luminosity that erased its previously distinct boundaries. The air was made of the same luminosity, which stretched as far as the eye could see in all directions. I felt more and more non-localized, as if "I" was nowhere in particular in that glowing fog, but everywhere at once.

When I looked over at Claude, who was telling me some story about one of his patients, he appeared to be far away and unreachable through the vast luminosity. He turned to me briefly to be sure I was paying attention, then asked me if I was all right. "Fine," I responded weakly, "just fine." Panic was beginning to well up inside, and I couldn't risk saying more. Then the panic kicked in with a vengeance, and terrifying thoughts began arising in my mind. I was going insane, said those thoughts, losing my grip on reality, becoming non-functional. I turned to Claude and searched for a subject to talk about, anything to distract me from the experience of dissolving into the air.

We talked for a while about his brother's newest romantic interest—how old she was, how they had met—then Claude began a rather long and complicated story about an incident his brother had described to him the day before on the phone. As I settled back in my seat and listened, I tried to maintain a focus on his words in order to bring myself back to solid reality. But the sensation of being far away remained and was to continue for several days, as did the distinct perception that the air was infused with a glowing fog. This perceptual shift was so distressing that I was unable to do anything but deliberately and obsessively try to distract myself from what was happening.

When we arrived at Claude's parents' home, I excitedly announced my pregnancy and chatted animatedly with everyone about motherhood and child-rearing. In the next few days, I flung myself into the concerns of everyday life for the sole purpose of erasing and attempting to forget the perceptual shift that had occurred.

Around this time, another perceptual shift began manifesting itself in discrete incidents that lasted anywhere from several minutes to several hours. During these episodes, the world appeared to be one-dimensional, as if it were a movie set cut from cardboard with nothing behind it. The Parisian scenery appeared flat, empty, and cartoonlike, lacking dimension or solidity. In addition, all the distinct edges that had previously marked separations between things took on a fuzzy liquidity without clear delineation, flowing together in an oceanlike movement. Objects that had previously seemed stable appeared to be simultaneously larger and farther away, pulsating gently in a single motion of life, subsisting in their own perceptual strata that was unreachable to my astounded mind. Each time these shifts occurred, terror arose immediately and remained, even increased, throughout their duration.

I had no idea what was happening. I assumed only that pregnancy was affecting me in a most peculiar manner, and I was relieved beyond belief when the shifts would finally subside and I would return to what I thought of as my normal perceptual state. Far from preparing me for something more radical, these shifts terrified me. I became hypervigilant to all changes in my usual mode of perception in an attempt to isolate what might be causing them to occur. I ran through a long list of possibilities, from specific foods to the amount of sleep or exercise I was getting, but I was unable to identify anything that could consistently be instigating these changes. It was a complete mystery—and the mystery was about to deepen a thousandfold.

It was in the springtime that it happened. I was returning home to my apartment on the Left Bank after attending a class for pregnant women at the clinic across town where I would be having my baby six months from then. It was the first week of my fourth month of pregnancy, and I had just begun to feel the faintest stirring of my daughter's tiny movements, like being brushed by a feather from the inside. The month was May, and the sun felt warm on my head and face as I stood at the bus stop on the Avenue de la Grande Armée. I was in no hurry and had decided to take a bus instead of the *metro* in order to enjoy the lovely weather.

Several buses came and went before I finally saw the number 37 approaching down the wide avenue. Six or seven of us were waiting together at the stop, exchanging pleasantries about the weather and comments about the new advertising campaign that had been appearing on all the billboards. As the bus approached, we congregated expectantly near the curb. The bus lumbered to a halt, expelling the acrid odor of exhaust fumes and hot rubber into the warm spring air.

As I took my place in line, I suddenly felt my ears stop up like they do when the pressure changes inside an airplane as it makes its descent. I felt cut off from the scene before me, as if I were enclosed in a bubble, unable to act in any but the most mechanical manner. I lifted my right foot to step up into the bus and collided head-on with an invisible force that entered my awareness like a silently exploding stick of dynamite, blowing the door of my usual consciousness open and off its hinges, splitting me in two. In the gaping space that appeared, what I had previously called "me" was forcefully pushed out of its usual location inside me into a new location that was approximately a foot behind and to the left of my head. "I" was now behind my body looking out at the world without using the body's eyes.

From a non-localized position somewhere behind and to the left, I could see my body in front and very far away. All the body's signals seemed to take a long time to be picked up in this non-localized place, as if they were light coming from a distant star. Terrified, I looked around, wondering if anyone else had noticed something. All the other passengers were calmly taking their seats, and the bus driver was motioning me to put my yellow ticket into the machine so we could be off.

I shook my head a few times, hoping to rattle my consciousness back into place, but nothing changed. I felt from afar as my fingers fumbled to insert the ticket into the slot and I walked down the aisle to find a seat. I sat down next to an older woman I had been chatting with at the bus stop, and I tried to continue our conversation. My mind had completely ground to a halt in the shock of the abrupt collision with whatever had dislodged my previous reality.

Although my voice continued speaking coherently, I felt completely disconnected from it. The face of the woman next to me seemed far away, and the air between us seemed foggy, as if filled with a thick, luminous soup. She turned to gaze out the window for a moment, then reached up to pull the cord to signal the driver to let her off at the next stop. When she rose, I slid over into her seat by the window and bid her goodbye with a smile. I could feel sweat rolling down my arms and beading up on my face. I was terrified.

The bus arrived at my stop on the rue Lecourbe, and I got off. As I walked the three blocks home, I attempted to pull myself back into one piece by focusing on my body and willing myself back into it where I thought I belonged in order to regain the previously normal sensation of seeing through the body's eyes, speaking through the body's mouth, and hearing through the body's ears. The force of will failed miserably. Instead of experiencing through the physical senses, I was now bobbing behind the body like a buoy on the sea. Cut loose from sensory solidity, separated from and witnessing the body from a vast distance, I moved down the street like a cloud of awareness following a body that seemed simultaneously familiar and foreign. There was an incomprehensible attachment to that body, although it no longer felt like "mine." It continued to send out signals of its sensory perceptions, yet how or where those signals were being received was beyond comprehension.

Incapable of making sense of this state, the mind alternated between racing wildly in an attempt to put "me" back together and shutting down completely, leaving only the empty humming of space reverberating in the ears. The witness was absolutely distinct from the mind, the body, and the emotions, and the position it held, behind and to the left of the head, remained constant. The profound distance between the witness and the mind, body, and emotions seemed to elicit panic in and of itself, due to the sensation of being so tenuously tethered to physical existence. In this witnessing state, physical existence was experienced to be on the verge of dissolution, and it (the physical) responded by summoning an annihilation fear of monumental proportions.

As I walked into my apartment, Claude looked up from his book to greet me and ask how my day had been. The terror was not immediately apparent to him, which seemed oddly reassuring. I greeted him calmly as if nothing were wrong, telling him about the class at the clinic and showing him the new book I had purchased at the American bookstore on my way home. There was no conceivable way to explain any of this to him, so I didn't even try. The terror was escalating rapidly, and the body was panic stricken, sweat pouring in rivulets down its sides, hands cold and trembling, heart pumping furiously. The mind clicked into survival mode and started looking for distractions. Maybe if I took a bath or a nap, or ate some food, or read a book, or called someone on the phone.

The whole thing was nightmarish beyond belief. The mind (I could no longer even call it "my" mind) was trying to come up with some explanation for this clearly inexplicable occurrence. The body moved beyond terror into a frenzied horror, giving rise to such utter physical exhaustion that sleep became the only possible option. After telling Claude that I didn't want to be disturbed, I lay down in bed and fell into what I thought would be the welcome oblivion of sleep. Sleep came, but the witness continued, witnessing sleep from its position behind the body. This was the oddest experience. The mind was definitely asleep, but something was simultaneously awake.

The moment the eyes opened the next morning, the mind exploded in worry. Is this insanity? Psychosis? Schizophrenia? Is this what people call a nervous breakdown? Depression? What had happened? And would it ever stop? Claude had started to notice my agitation and was apparently waiting for an explanation. I attempted to tell him what had taken place the day before, but I was just too far away to speak. The witness appeared to be where "I" was located, which left the body, mind, and emotions empty of a person. It was amazing that all those functions continued to operate at all. There was no explaining this one to Claude, and for once I was glad he was the kind of person who didn't persist in pursuing a subject I didn't want to pursue.

The mind was so overwhelmed by its inability to comprehend the current state of existence that it could not be distracted. It remained riveted to the incomprehensible, unanswerable quandaries that were generated in an unbroken stream out of this witnessing state of awareness. There was the sense of being on an edge of sorts, a boundary between existing and not existing, and the mind believed that if it did not maintain the thought of existence, existence itself would cease. Charged with this apparently life-or-death directive, the mind struggled to hold that thought, only to exhaust itself after several fitful hours. The mind was in agony as it tried valiantly to make sense of something it could never comprehend, and the body responded to the anguish of the mind by locking itself into survival mode, adrenaline pumping, senses fine-tuned, finding and responding to the threat of annihilation in every moment.

The thought did arise that perhaps this experience of witnessing was the state of Cosmic Consciousness Maharishi had described long before as the first stage of awakened awareness. But the mind instantly discarded this possibility because it seemed impossible that the hell realm I was inhabiting could have anything to do with Cosmic Consciousness.

━━━

The witnessing persisted for months, and each moment was excruciating. Living on the verge of dissolution for weeks on end is stressful beyond belief, and the only respite was the oblivion of sleep into which I plunged for as long and as often as possible. In sleep, the mind finally stopped pumping out its unceasing litany of terror, and the witness was left to witness an unconscious mind.

After months of this mystifying witness awareness, something changed yet again: The witness disappeared. This new state was far more baffling, and
consequently more terrifying, than the experience of
the preceding months. One might imagine that a
great weight would have lifted when the witness disappeared, but the opposite was true. The disappearance of the witness meant the disappearance of the
last vestiges of the experience of personal identity.
The witness had at least held a location for a "me,"
albeit a distant one. In the dissolution of the witness,
there was literally no more experience of a "me" at all.
The experience of personal identity switched off and
was never to appear again.

The personal self was gone, yet here was a body
and a mind that still existed empty of anyone who
occupied them. The experience of living without a
personal identity, without an experience of being
somebody, an "I" or a "me," is exceedingly difficult to
describe, but it is absolutely unmistakable. It can't be
confused with having a bad day or coming down with
the flu or feeling upset or angry or spaced out. When
the personal self disappears, there is no one inside
who can be located as being you. The body is only an
outline, empty of everything of which it had previously felt so full.

The mind, body, and emotions no longer
referred to anyone—there was no one who thought,
no one who felt, no one who perceived. Yet the
mind, body, and emotions continued to function
unimpaired; apparently they did not need an "I" to
keep doing what they always did. Thinking, feeling,
perceiving, speaking, all continued as before, func-

tioning with a smoothness that gave no indication of the emptiness behind them. No one suspected that such a radical change had occurred. All conversations were carried on as before; language was employed in the same manner. Questions could be asked and answered, cars driven, meals cooked, books read, phones answered, and letters written. Everything appeared completely normal from the outside, as if the same old Suzanne was going about her life as she always had.

In an attempt to understand what had occurred, the mind began working overtime, generating endless questions, all unanswerable. Who thought? Who felt? Who was afraid? Who were people talking to when they spoke to me? Who were they looking at? Why was there a reflection in the mirror, since there was no one there? Why did these eyes open in the morning? Why did this body continue? Who was living? Life became one long, unbroken koan, forever unsolvable, forever mysterious, completely out of reach of the mind's capacity to comprehend.

The oddest moments occurred when any reference was made to my name. If I had to write it on a check or sign it on a letter, I would stare at the letters on the paper and the mind would drown in perplexity. The name referred to no one. There was no Suzanne Segal anymore; perhaps there never had been. There is a turning inward that occurs when the mind searches for internal information, whether it be about feelings or thoughts or connection to a name or inner experience of any kind. This is generally referred to as introspection. Without a personal self, the inside or internal simply did not exist. The inward-turning motion of the mind became the most bizarre of experiences when time and again it found total emptiness where it had previously found an object to perceive, a self-concept.

The more baffled the mind became, the greater the fear. By this time, the body had locked into a pitch of terror that generated continuous shaking in the extremities and copious sweating. My clothing was constantly damp, and the sheets on the bed needed to be hung out to dry every morning. Worst of all, simultaneous with the cessation of personal identity, the experience of sleep had changed radically, leaving me with no escape from the constant awareness of emptiness of self. Sleeping and dreaming now contained the awareness of no one who slept or dreamed, just as the waking state of consciousness contained the awareness that there was no one who was awake.

At this point it became necessary to attempt to describe to Claude what was happening. He had noticed a distinct increase in my level of anxiety and agitation and had been trying for months to get me to talk.

"Something has happened to me, Claude," I began in French, trying to choose words carefully. "I have no idea what it is but...I feel like I don't exist anymore. There's no more 'me,' no more personal identity. It started months ago when I was on my way home from the class at the clinic. I was getting on the bus and something just changed, and now—

well, I just can't seem to find an experience of a person in me like I used to.

"You know how you never have any doubts about who you are, like if someone says to you 'Who are you?' and you just know, 'I'm me, of course.' Well, I can't find a 'me' anymore. There's no one."

"What do you mean there's no more you?" he said. "Of course there's a you. Here you are right in front of me, talking to me."

"But I don't experience a 'me' anymore," I practically shouted. "It's the most horrible thing that has ever happened. When I look in the mirror, I'm shocked to see a reflection. When I walk down the street and people look at me, I wonder who they're looking at. When I talk, I hear a voice speaking, but there's no one behind the voice. Oh, this is impossible to explain to you. It just can't be put into words, but it's awful! Maybe I've gone completely insane. Is that possible?"

"Suzanne, try to calm down. Let's make an appointment to take you to a psychiatrist, all right? Do you think that would help?"

"I have no idea," I replied, now literally vibrating with fear. "None of this makes any sense. How can everything just go on as before, still talking and walking, sleeping and dreaming, crying and laughing, but no 'me' doing any of it?"

Claude obviously had no answer. After asking a few more questions, he walked out of the room to make an appointment with a psychiatrist who was recommended by one of his colleagues. He came with me to the appointed hour and sat silently as I explained everything to the doctor, exchanging worried looks with him as my story unfolded. It was not easy to find the words in French to describe this state, and the psychiatrist kept staring at me in the most perplexed manner. I told him about the witnessing and the luminous fogginess. I described as well as I could the experience of feeling like there was no person left inside, that the sense of having a personal identity had ceased and that it seemed like it was never going to return. I told him about the terror that would not stop and how there was no one who felt the terror, even though the body and mind kept generating it. I told him that my name didn't refer to anyone anymore. When I finished my story, he fumbled for something to say.

"I don't know what to tell you," he began. "I'm not sure what's wrong with you, but I can give you some medicine to help you calm your anxiety. Since you're pregnant, I can't give you anything strong. But once you have the baby we'll try to find the appropriate medication for you. Something has apparently happened to your mind that may become more serious if you don't take some medication fairly soon."

"But what has happened? Where did 'I' go? Will 'I' ever come back?" I blurted out, "Have you ever heard of anything like this before?"

He just shook his head and rose to his feet, signaling that our meeting was over. As we walked to the door, I turned to see him shaking hands with Claude and patting him sympathetically on the shoulder.

"*Bon courage*," he said as he opened the door, clearly eager to be rid of us. "Good luck. Call me when you have the baby to let me know how you're doing."

Claude looked at me sadly, knowing there was nothing more to say.

Shortly after the visit to the psychiatrist, thoughts about my mother began circulating obsessively in the mind. If only I could see my mother, the thoughts said, everything would be all right. All I needed was to lay eyes on her, the woman who bore me, who raised me, who named me. I became convinced that seeing her was going to provide a cure for this strange malady by restoring my personal identity. The mind was still trying desperately to figure out a way to get back the experience of a 'me.'

Claude agreed to accompany me on the flight to Chicago. Because I was in my seventh month of pregnancy by then, the trip needed to happen right away. I called my mother and my brother Dan and arranged for them to pick us up at the airport. During the flight the mind generated fantasies about its imminent release from the nightmarish experience of trying to comprehend the cessation of personal identity. Claude remarked that he was happy to see a smile on my face for the first time in months. We touched down at O'Hare Airport and made our way to the baggage terminal to collect our suitcases. The mind kept insisting that everything would return to normal as soon as I saw my mom.

As we stepped off the escalator, there she was. She was smaller than I remembered, and she had dyed her hair blonde. The moment I saw her, my heart sank. The sight of her did nothing, changed nothing in the emptiness. "I" was still not there. She ran up and hugged me, then pulled back to search my face for a smile, but there was none. In that moment a deep despair settled over the mind as it realized that I would never again experience having a personal self—even though the mind could never grasp how that was possible.

My mother started to tell me about the fascinating people she was spending time with and all the interesting things she was doing. She glanced at me from time to time but did not seem to notice that something was wrong. I couldn't bring myself to speak so I simply stared at her in silence, nodding once in a while to make it look like I was following what she was saying. I caught my brother's attention and signaled to him that I wanted to talk. He and I walked to the baggage carousel to wait for the luggage, and I began describing what had been happening, but I couldn't say much before my mother and Claude joined us. We gathered our bags and walked to the car for the drive home.

As we made our way through the familiar suburbs of Chicago, scores of unanswerable questions flooded the mind. Who recognizes this scenery? Who knows that we should turn left here or right there? Who are these people in the car? I kept looking at my mother and brother, wondering who they were. Everything was at once totally familiar and totally foreign. There was no longer anything that felt like "connection" since there was no one to be connected to. How would relationships occur now that there was no person to have them?

By the time we arrived at my mother's house, it was obvious to everyone that I was not doing well. My mother, who was sitting next to me in the back seat, kept patting my hand, telling me how hard pregnancy was, and reassuring me that it would soon be over. Dan, who was driving, kept glancing back at me with concern in the rear-view mirror. I answered his look with a look of my own and shrugged my shoulders. He fixed me with a searching gaze, then turned the car into the driveway and shut off the engine. We all sat in silence for several minutes before Claude opened his door and got out. My mother turned to me and started to cry. My brother reached over the seat and patted her on the shoulder. I said nothing.

As we fixed dinner, my mother maintained a steady patter of gossip, stories, and musings. Then she and Claude struck up a conversation about his family and our life in Paris, which left Dan and me free to speak in private. I hurriedly described my experience to him, beginning with the bus stop and ending with the current state of no-self, which was so utterly perturbing to the mind. He told me that he occasionally had a similar experience, which he characterized as a "spaciness" in which he was unable to relate to having a body or to feel like he was really there. He said he just went on about his life without paying much attention to it. I replied that I would not describe this experience as spaciness—I would describe it as having ceased to be someone.

After dinner my younger brother, Bob, arrived from his home in downtown Chicago to spend the evening with us. He had been involved in primal therapy for several years, and when he heard my story, he suggested I see his therapist, Paul. I agreed, since the fear seemed to be steadily increasing, and along with it the renewed concern that this experience was a sign of insanity. The sensation of constantly being on the verge of dissolution was intensely taxing to the mind and body, which led the mind to the apparently logical conclusion that a complete breakdown of functioning was imminent. The thought that someone could stave off this imminent breakdown, or even provide a modicum of reassurance, was attractive, to say the least. Bob set up an appointment for the following day and wrote out directions to Paul's office on a slip of paper.

The experience of describing the cessation of personal identity to a psychotherapist was one that I would repeat many times in the next ten years. Paul was clearly a kind-hearted man, eager to help in any way he could. Yet he was utterly mystified by what I was telling him, and his mystification seemed to make him afraid—certainly not a useful response for me. By the time I left his office my body was stiff with terror. I went to my mother's house, closed the drapes in my bedroom, and slept for thirteen hours.

The next day my mother had planned a party in my honor, to which she had invited many of her old friends who had known me since I was a child and who were thrilled to be celebrating my impending motherhood. Thirty people gathered in the late afternoon at a well-known suburban restaurant. As each guest approached me to offer their congratulations, I tried to behave like a normal human being, shaking hands and smiling, inquiring about their health or their children. How did I know these people? Who remembered their names and all the years spent visiting with them exchanging stories of our lives? The person they had previously known no longer existed, but no one seemed to notice.

The return to Paris marked the beginning of true despair. I walked around wondering who was still alive. I wandered the streets gazing into every shop window, praying that the next glimpse of my reflection would bring back a flicker of recognition, praying for a solid experience of seeing myself in the eyes that stared back from the window's glare. It never happened.

In addition to the absence of self, the filters that had previously screened out the constant sensory input of the world had ceased to function. I could no longer venture into stores or other crowded places because the sensory stimulation seemed to overload the now delicate circuits of an already overtaxed brain. The mind was struggling to hold onto the thought of my existence, since, in the mind's view, my very existence depended on it. With too much stimulation, the mind was unable to hold that thought, and a horrifying fear of annihilation would ensue.

Everything appeared to be dissolving right in front of my eyes, constantly. Emptiness was everywhere, seeping through the pores of every face I gazed upon, flowing through the crevices of seemingly solid objects. The body, mind, speech, thoughts, and emotions were all empty; they had no ownership, no person behind them. I was utterly bereft of all my previous notions of reality.

While I was still a college student in California, I had consulted a well-known psychologist who was also an avid devotee of Meher Baba, and I had come to trust his views of both the spiritual and the psychological realms. Now I decided to give him a call. I finally managed to track him down at a university on the East Coast where he was working for the summer. He was surprised to hear my voice and amazed that I had located him. I described my experience—the witnessing, the space, the emptiness, the absence of personal identity—and pleaded with him to help me

understand what was going on and to reassure me
that I hadn't lost my mind. He listened carefully and
asked several clarifying questions. Then, to my disbelief, he congratulated me.

"How wonderful!" he exclaimed. "People spend
years in caves trying to get this experience. You get
consciousness gold stars all over the place for this one!"

"But Alan," I cried, "you don't understand. This
couldn't be a spiritual awakening. This feels horrible.
I want it to go away. I'm terrified all the time, and I
want to go back to being how I was before."

"Take Baba's name and repeat it," he said. "Things
will be better."

He reassured me that this was by no means a
pathological state, that I shouldn't worry, that it was
truly a much sought-after spiritual experience. Yet it
was impossible to believe him, because every idea I
had ever acquired about spiritual development was
based solely on notions of bliss and ecstasy. It seemed
inconceivable that a genuine spiritual experience
could be as horrifying as the state I found myself in.

"If this is what people spend years in caves trying
to achieve," I told him, "they're out of their minds."

In November 1982 my daughter was born. The
labor and birth took a total of three days, and the
exhaustion was beyond anything I had ever known.
Yet even such an extremity of physical and emotional
fatigue did not overshadow the experience of no-self,
which was as omnipresent as ever. During childbirth
it became utterly clear that all of life is accomplished

by an unseen doer who can never be located. The previous sense of an "I" who was doing was totally illusory. The personal "I" had never been the doer—it had only masqueraded as the doer. Everything continued as before, only the person who used to think she was doing was absent.

The horror the mind encountered when it was forced into direct, unceasing contact with the vastness of no reference point had given rise to the concern that pregnancy would not continue or that birth would never happen because there was now no one there to do it. It seemed so unimaginable that everything would continue as before now that it was all seen to be empty of what it had previously been full of. But continue it did, just as before—and in most cases even better. The birth of my daughter occurred with all of the sensations, emotions, and thoughts that are present during any birth. There was wondering about the health of the infant; concern about the intensity of sensation; anxiety about knowing how to care for a newborn; and awe at the mystery of it all.

The clinic in Paris where I went to give birth had been started by Frederic Lamaze. It was a Communist Labor Party clinic in a gritty part of the city that employed midwives almost exclusively. There was one doctor on duty during each eight-hour shift, but I never saw him.

When the contractions began, Claude drove me to the clinic, and one of the midwives examined me. She said that I should go home again and come back when the contractions were two minutes apart. We drove home and waited, but they never changed from their five-minute pattern, so eight hours later we drove back to the clinic. The midwife again examined me and told me to wait. She went off to consult with someone, then returned to say she had arranged a place for me to rest. She led us upstairs to a tiny room where I lay down on a table and waited for the next wave of contractions to begin.

The constant presence of the emptiness was not something I could mention to anyone there. Claude had heard all he was going to hear about it. In fact, he had made it clear weeks before that he didn't want to discuss that "craziness" anymore. The mind kept up its constant attempts to locate a someone to whom all of this was happening. When it failed again and again, it cranked up the terror with its bleak scenarios of what was certain to occur since "I" no longer existed. I mean, how can you have a baby if you don't exist? During this stage of labor, the mind kept saying that the birth would never take place unless someone was found who could give birth. Yet all the birthing functions were functioning—albeit slowly.

Claude asked the midwives if he could try some acupuncture on me to help make the contractions more effective. Everyone was interested in seeing this little experiment, so he got out his needles and electrical stimulation equipment and went to work. He placed about twenty-five needles in several of the meridians on both sides of the body and attached the electric stimulators to each needle. As soon as he turned on the electricity, the contractions intensified significantly. The four midwives who were present seemed to be impressed with the results. The stronger contractions continued for twenty minutes, then the head midwife checked to see if more dilation had occurred. It had not.

Although the contractions were significantly stronger with the needles in place, they were no more effective than before.

A decision was then made to put me on pitocin, which is a drug used to induce labor. I was told that if the baby wasn't born within six hours after they gave me the pitocin, they would have to do a cesarean. The intravenous device was hooked up, and within forty minutes the contractions were immense in their power. In another forty-five minutes they were coming every minute and were highly effective in increasing dilation. Three hours after the pitocin was administered, the baby started to move into the birth canal, and forty minutes later she was born.

In accordance with the views of Frederic LeBoyer, whose philosophy this clinic was the first to adopt, my daughter was birthed in a darkened room, so she wouldn't be shocked by bright lights, into a large basin filled with warm water to ease the transition into the world outside the womb.

How can one describe a baby being born to no one? She had no mother, yet the birth occurred just fine, and in the years to come the mothering function would take care of her and raise her in a completely competent manner. The mind never stopped questioning how mothering could occur without anyone there to do it, but the mind was forced to witness mothering mother without hesitation.

The birth had taken nearly three days, during which the body had experienced intense contractions at regular intervals and had barely slept, and the physical functioning was exhausted. I was put into a room in the clinic with another woman who had had her baby the day before. In France, new mothers are kept for one week in the clinic after giving birth. Both of the babies were with us, since the Lamaze philosophy dictates that infants should not be separated from their mothers after birth.

For the first week I didn't sleep more than two hours at a stretch. Either one baby or the other was awake almost constantly, and the exhaustion was deepening significantly. The way the body experienced exhaustion did not change in the face of no reference point. Nor is it different now—the body's functioning still requires what it has always required in terms of rest, nourishment, and care.

The first year of my daughter's life was both exhausting and exhilarating. At first she didn't seem to require much sleep, which was not unusual for a newborn, although the adult body found it intolerable at times to go for so long without regular sleep. The less sleep the body received, the more the mind became enthusiastically convinced that insanity was the truth of what had occurred in the aftermath of the bus stop—especially since there was simultaneously an extremity of emptiness that deepened in its starkness as the body accumulated exhaustion.

Nevertheless, the relationship between my daughter, Arielle, and her mother who is no one developed so beautifully that the mind was inevitably foiled in its attempts to pathologize the emptiness of personal self or interpret it as insanity. Everyone who observed our relationship directly or knew Arielle in some other context agreed that she was an extraordinary child who showed no signs of being traumatized in any way.

Since no one could tell from the outside that I was having this remarkably different experience, I was able to "fool" everyone into thinking that I was just as I used to be. My in-laws were thrilled with their new granddaughter, and they celebrated the occasion in high spirits, organizing a large party to welcome her into the family. Although waves of fear continued to crash unceasingly through my awareness, the perfectly normal functioning of what everyone took to be the "normal" Suzanne continued unperturbed. No one noticed anything awry in my comportment as they merrily filed by to admire my daughter and extend their heartfelt congratulations. How extraordinary! the mind thought. My daughter will never have a mother. There is no one here, and it's apparently unnecessary to be someone for mothering to take place. Mothering mothers, just as talking talks and thinking thinks. The mind was having a hard time getting used to this.

When my daughter was eight months old, I realized that it was time to leave Paris. Claude made every attempt to dissuade me, but I knew that returning to the United States was simply and clearly the next thing to be done. Although a little over a year had elapsed since the "I" had shattered, the relentlessness of no-self was still far from adjusted to. My relationship to Claude had changed dramatically as I struggled to understand an utterly inconceivable experience that Claude could certainly not be expected to grasp. Over time our relationship had virtually dissolved. The person he had married was no longer there. I was no longer able to have "personal" relationships, and never would be again.

Claude made the decision to come with me in an attempt to keep our family together. As a physician in France, he had to pass an examination and spend a year in an internship to be considered a licensed doctor in the United States. In the months before we left, he began studying seriously for the exam as I began the task of packing up our lives in Paris for the move back. Claude's family was terribly sad at the news of our leaving, but they did nothing to try to dissuade us. They were all aware that I was having difficulties in Paris, although they had no idea why. They probably hoped that a change of scenery would help me feel happier. I suppose the consensus on my problem was that I was depressed and homesick, and I'm certain they prayed that our marriage would improve.

My daughter was not the least upset by anything. She was a delightful, happy child who was constantly impressing people with her precociousness. She was able to laugh in the face of any challenge, dimpling her cheeks and shaking her blonde curls until everyone around her was charmed into forgetting their sadness. I was relieved to see her so happy, since I had repeatedly wondered whether the terror and the radical shift of consciousness that had accompanied the last five months of my pregnancy had left any problematic impressions on her.

Whatever impressions may have been left did not appear to have traumatized her. As she has matured into a teenager, she has continued to exude the wise happiness that has always radiated from her since the day she was born. In fact, she has frequently expressed a clear knowing that she is both different from and the same as other people. At times she finds this confusing, and generally she would rather not speak about it. But on at least one occasion she has said, "You know, Mom, when people look at you and they think you're someone, but you know you're not that person?"

"Yes, sweetheart," I've answered, "I do know that experience."

5.

DEVALUING EMPTINESS

I have lived on the lip
of insanity, wanting to know reasons,
knocking on a door. It opens.
I've been knocking from the inside!
        —Rumi

In the spring of 1984, nearly two years after the experience of no-self began, we left Paris and returned to the Chicago area because I hoped that living in familiar surroundings might be helpful in calming the fear. But it was not to be so. Being around my family, particularly my mother, was distressing. She perceived me as profoundly depressed and repeatedly insisted that I see her psychiatrist for a medication evaluation. Although I was able to avoid the psychiatrist, it was harder to avoid the look of hopelessness and sadness in my mother's eyes each time we met.

Returning to the United States, to my mother's home, brought me face to face with the fear of insanity. She symbolized the Western world's inclination to accept only reasonable, understandable experiences as valid. What I was experiencing made no scientific or psychological sense, and therefore it was considered pathological.

I resolved not to speak to anyone else about my experience. I would just get on with my life and forget that I no longer had a self. It was an absurd resolution, of course, since having no self is not something one can just put out of one's mind. But everything seemed absurd at that point. After all, how many people were living without an experience of having a personal identity?

The mind was clearly having a hard time with the experience of no-self. It appeared to be on a campaign to prove that something was seriously wrong, and it employed any available evidence to substantiate this belief. The most compelling piece of evidence was the presence of terror. Every description I'd ever heard of spiritual development had included some mention of bliss, ecstasy, or joy. But there was no bliss in this experience of no-self. When the mind turned inward again and again to locate an experiencer, a self-concept, it repeatedly generated terror as it found only emptiness.

Relationships to other people had been radically altered. Without a personal "I," there was nowhere for the reverberations of experience to be received. The feeling of being connected to others was gone because there was no longer a person to whom they could be connected. I must reiterate, however, that all feelings continued to arise appropriately. What had vanished was the reference point of a personal self that felt the feelings personally. Emptiness was consistently co-present with all emotional or mental states, and this co-presence precluded any personal quality from existing. No thoughts, feelings, or actions arose for any personal purpose anymore.

The strangest phenomenon of all was the fact of having no name—literally. The name by which I had been identified now corresponded to no one. Seeing that name written down stimulated no current of recognition; hearing that name spoken produced no sense of the person to whom it referred. To this day, an intensification of emptiness still occurs when that name is spoken or written. This intensification is experienced as a deepening of emptiness, like a void turning in to look at itself and in that glance being reminded of how empty it really is.

Many years later, the mind did recall the childhood practice of repeating my name until it led me to the frightening truth that I did not possess an individual identity. This memory brought some degree of peace, although the mind still refused to accept that the lack of personal identity was anything but pathological. The best that could be hoped for, it seemed, was that the mind would eventually become accustomed to this state and stop conveying the message that something was horribly wrong. But this would not occur for more than a decade.

In the year after our return to the United States, Claude successfully passed the medical exam and was accepted into an internship at Cook County Hospital in Chicago. Before he could begin the internship, however, the strain of living in a relationship that was irrevocably changed, and in a foreign country that did not prove altogether hospitable, became too much for him to bear. We decided to separate in January of 1985, and Claude moved into an apartment near downtown Chicago where he lived for six months before we were officially divorced. In September, two months after our marriage ended, he left the country, heartbroken and disappointed, to begin a new life in a more familiar and supportive environment.

I can only say that I felt no sadness at his departure. Our relationship had ceased to exist two years before, when it became clear that he had no further interest in being a partner to such a perplexing mystery. We agreed that our daughter would remain with me in the United States and would visit with him in Paris several times a year. By the time Claude left, I was making plans to move back to California. It was the next obvious thing to do.

Around the time Claude and I were separating, my brother Dan told me about a spiritual teacher he had discovered who had allegedly become enlightened during a TM teacher-training course in Switzerland. Robert Peterson was a charismatic Canadian man whose reputation as a rebel and iconoclast was attracting attention throughout the TM community, particularly in Fairfield, Iowa, where the Maharishi International University was located. Thinking that Robert might be a good person for me to meet, Dan arranged for me to join him on a trip to Fairfield.

About sixty people had gathered, and as soon as Dan and I walked into the room, Robert asked me to come up to the microphone to dialogue with him.

"Welcome, Suzanne," Robert said enthusiastically. "Tell me about yourself and your life."

"Well, I just returned from Paris where I was living

for three and a half years. I became a TM teacher in 1975, but I haven't been meditating for the past six years. I hear that you're doing some interesting work with people who have been disappointed with Maharishi's teachings."

"I guess that's true, but most importantly I've been bringing the drama of the light of consciousness to everyone. I must tell you that it's very clear how special you are. I feel very strongly that you should leave wherever you are and come to live in my community in Victoria. You are very, very special. Please, Suzanne, can you come to be with me?"

"I don't know, Robert, I suppose I can consider it. Canada? Maybe..."

We spoke for some minutes more, then a group of his followers surrounded me and told me they had never before heard Robert make such a direct request to anyone to join him. I said I would consider his offer, since there didn't appear to be anything holding me elsewhere.

As we traveled back to Chicago the next day, Dan and I discussed the possibility at length. I decided to ask my mother if she would be willing to take care of Arielle for a few days while I flew to Victoria to check things out. She readily agreed, and I made plans to leave two weeks later.

Arriving at the tiny Victoria airport on a nine-passenger shuttle from Seattle, I was met by a friend of my brother's, who had invited me to stay at his house while I was in town. The next morning we left early to attend Robert's weekend course, which he was offering in a lecture hall of the university in town.

It was exciting to see Robert again. The group of people who surrounded him were all mesmerized by his charisma. He presented his teachings with such power that their actual content mattered little. His best friend and right-hand man, William, welcomed me enthusiastically, and it soon became apparent that William and I were drawn to each other.

During the weekend I listened closely for any possibility of talking to someone about my experience of no-self. Although this was the first spiritual environment I had encountered since the emptiness of personal self had occurred, it did not seem to be a hospitable one for a discussion of the no-self experience. After all, Robert was a follower of Maharishi Mahesh Yogi, who had never mentioned no-self in any of his teachings. The mind continued to generate a great deal of fear about the emptiness, which was not diminished on hearing what Robert had to say.

In the five months that followed, I shuttled back and forth between Victoria and Chicago. Since Claude and I were in the process of divorcing, discussions with an attorney in Chicago as well as visits between Claude and Arielle needed to be arranged. But when there were breaks in those responsibilities, Arielle and I would fly to Victoria.

Within a few weeks of spending more regular time with Robert, William and I became lovers, and I was invited to move into his apartment, which was located on the first floor of a beautiful house owned by a group of Robert's students. The relationship with William occurred out of the same emptiness that was always present as the non-locatable doer. Becoming lovers was simply the next obvious thing to do, but it did not arise out of personal need or desire. The functions that operate in relationship continued to operate, even though there was no one to whom they referred. Nothing proceeded on the basis of reasons why or decisions about whether. There was no longer anything resembling a choice-maker, one who appeared to decide whether a relationship should or shouldn't happen or whether the person was or was not an appropriate partner. Even though the relationship appeared to be personal, it was not, and the mind found this confounding and frightening.

Robert had a tradition of "confronting" his students when he thought they had done something wrong. As I listened to more and more of his talks, it became clear that he was seeing the world and everyone in it in terms of good and evil. When he confronted someone, he based his attack on seeing that they were evil, and they were ostracized from the community immediately after the confrontation. Some people had been confronted, ostracized, then brought back many times over the years. Others were confronted, then left the community for good.

One day a woman who had been labeled "psychotic" by Robert arrived for a week-long course. She was attractive, and she spoke coherently and lucidly about a variety of topics. No one but Robert perceived her to be "crazy." In Robert's view, in fact, craziness and evil were synonymous. The woman was asked to stand in front of the group of students and describe her experience. She stood nervously and said, "My problem is a profound lack of self."

Hearing this statement made my blood run cold. It was the worst verification I had ever heard that the emptiness was what the fear proclaimed it to be: insanity. Robert responded to the woman's description by telling how he had "cured" her the previous evening by "giving her back a self." She agreed that this had occurred and expressed her immense gratitude to him. He smiled and proudly accepted her praise.

Now terror set in with a vengeance. Three days later, William and I stayed up all night talking about how terrified I was (even though I never described my experience of no-self to him), and he suggested we meet with Robert. I said I couldn't imagine that Robert would be awake then, since it was about four-thirty in the morning, but William insisted we call. Robert answered the phone and told us to come over to his house right away. We arrived about ten minutes later, and he met us with a big smile. We talked together for an hour, mostly about whatever it was that Robert had on his mind at the time. Then William and I left.

One week later, while William was out of town for two days, Robert called me late one night. He said he had felt strange ever since our talk the previous week, and he wondered what I had done to him. This was the kind of accusation that Robert often leveled at others. Whenever he felt "dissociated, spacy, or dissolved" in someone's presence, he concluded that the person must be evil. William had said something similar to me once before. Upon awakening from a late-afternoon nap together, he had wondered what I had done to him in his sleep that kept him from feeling good after awakening.

Robert and I hung up the phone, and I fell asleep. At six in the morning, Tessa, Robert's wife, came into my room and woke me. She said that Robert was outside in the entryway and wanted to speak with me. What she didn't tell me was that Robert had been telling the other students in the house that I was evil because I was Jewish. The previous week, apparently, he had come to the dramatic realization that all Jews were evil. Now he was meeting in the front hallway with some of his long-time students, urging them to get me out of the house.

I met Robert in the entryway, and he asked me to follow him into one of the other student's apartments to talk. There I found twelve people who had come to witness our conversation. He started by accusing me of making him feel "strange" the previous week, then proceeded to enumerate all the things I had done to him. Finally he told me I needed to leave right away because all Jews were evil and therefore were no longer welcome in this house, which was a sacred place for him.

I was sent to my room to pack my things, and it was arranged that Arielle and I would take over the apartment of another student who lived several miles away. I wanted to wait until William returned to see how he would take this news, but I wasn't allowed to remain in the house for more than an hour. I packed quickly and was transported to the new apartment by two men from the house.

When William returned the following day, he was intercepted by the household to inform him of the previous day's events. He never came to see me and never called to find out how I was doing. Robert had warned him to have nothing to do with me.

Within a week I made arrangements to leave Victoria. As I was planning the return to the States, I found out that Robert had confronted William and accused him of being the devil himself.

The drama of Robert's relationship to what he termed evil was used by the mind as powerful evidence against the emptiness of personal self. Since this was the first spiritual community I had encountered since the abrupt dropping away of personal identity nearly three years before, the mind concluded that all spiritual teachings would consider my experience pathological, as Robert had. Understandably, there was no appeal in turning again to the spiritual realm for help in making sense of this mysterious state.

During the final week of my stay in Victoria, I learned that my father had died. Since returning from Paris, I had visited him frequently at the nursing home where he had been living for the previous six months. For ten years he had suffered from Alzheimer's disease, and his inexorable decline had given further fuel to the incessant fear of the mind that functioning would cease or be greatly compromised in the emptiness of personal self.

After all, he had clearly been emptied of somebodyness, and look what had happened to him. He no longer recognized his children or his wife. He no longer knew who he was. He no longer spoke or read or drove or walked. Every glance in his direction cranked up the fear that I would soon end up just like him.

When I received the news of his death, I cried. There was no one who felt sad, yet the emotional response occurred as before and appeared to be about a someone, though it was not. Crying was there—simply that. To others it may have seemed that there was someone who was sad, but there was no one.

The mind did not take well to this continuation of emotional functioning in the face of no-self, and once again it began collecting evidence to show that something was wrong with the experience. At the same time, it tried to make it look like I was a someone who was responding appropriately to the death of her father. I flew back to Chicago immediately and helped my brothers and mother make arrangements for the funeral. In their presence I cried profusely and regularly whenever we spoke about our dad. The "attempt to be someone" was putting on a convincing performance, and I told no one that all those emotions never for a moment referred to a "me."

6.

ANALYZING EMPTINESS

Anxious, we keep longing for a foothold—
we, at times too young for what is old
and too old for what has never been...
            —Rainer Maria Rilke

My daughter and I set out for San Francisco in January 1986. We rented an apartment on the top floor of a beautifully restored Victorian in a quiet neighborhood and settled into a comfortable routine of lazy mornings, long afternoons in the park, and evenings of story-reading bundled together on the living room couch. The first weeks passed quickly in this manner, providing a welcome respite from the previous months, which had centered on divorce proceedings, intense confrontations, and my father's death.

Arielle continued to be a delightful companion, her easy laughter tumbling forth endlessly, transforming every situation into a wonderful adventure. Her presence was soothing to the fear that continued to hold my experience in its grip now three years after that fateful encounter with emptiness. I came to depend on her laughter to calm my mind when it was most enthusiastically generating its vast array of fearful ideas. She helped me more than anyone then, and for years afterwards, with her sweet reminders that safety can be found in even the most terrifying of moments if you don't lose your sense of humor.

The process of growing accustomed to having no individual self continued to unfold. The mind watchfully monitored how differently the events of life were being experienced, noting and commenting (as minds do) upon the negatives and positives of each and every moment. Since the mind had already judged the entire shift of consciousness to be negative, there was little room for the positive to be perceived. In those rare moments when the emptiness appeared to move to the background, even slightly, the mind seized the opportunity to note a return to a "normal" state of awareness. This shifting of the emptiness to a background position was the only thing that qualified as positive to the mind.

The mind's hypervigilance was exhausting. Because it was constantly engaged in rejecting the experience of emptiness, there was very little attention available for anything else. My life was filled with seeing no-self, fearing no-self, judging no-self, trying to forget no-self, rejecting no-self, worrying about no-self, and raising questions about no-self. Even in sleep the emptiness of personal identity continued unperturbed. No mental activity ever changed the experience of no-self in any manner, and none of the attempts to figure out, organize, or evaluate it ever brought back a sense of an individual identity.

⟳

The mind seemed driven to understand what had occurred, but its search for answers within the mind itself was not yielding results. Consequently, the notion that someone else might explain this phenomenon began to predominate. Who might understand what had occurred? The fear of insanity was still the most prominent concern, and, although I had had no previous luck in finding a psychotherapist who could help me understand my experience, psychotherapy still seemed like the only place to turn.

A friend who worked at a suicide hotline told me about a psychiatrist who was treating one of the more frequent callers. The patient raved about his uncanny ability to help her find the humor in life—something my daughter had certainly shown me was vital. I called him to make an appointment and the following week drove the hour south to meet with him in his office in Los Gatos, near San Jose.

Carl Trimble's office was located in a small complex just off the highway that winds through the beautiful Santa Cruz mountains. He greeted me warmly and invited me to sit in one of the comfortable chairs opposite his wooden rocker. He lit his pipe and sat back, asking me how he could help me. I starting describing my experience to him, watching carefully for his reactions. He listened silently for some time and then raised several questions about my life in Paris, my marriage, and my feelings about being pregnant. I answered as fully as possible, aware that he was trying to evaluate whether there had been some particular stressor that might have given rise to the experience. I told him that my father had died just six months before, a fact that he noted on the pad in his lap where he was making occasional notes as we talked. I asked him if he had ever heard of an experience like this one before, and he said he had.

"You have?" I said hesitantly, with some anxiety in my voice. "Really? Well, what is it, exactly?"

"It's called depersonalization disorder," he said, without changing his expression. "It's common for people to have this experience after encountering a deep shock, like when someone they love dies, or they hear some really bad news, or even when something overwhelmingly positive happens, like they win the lottery. It usually comes and goes over a period of a few hours, or a few days at most. Frankly, I've never heard of it lasting as long as it has with you. But I'm sure that's what it is, and I'm certain I can help you with it."

"Help it to go away?" I asked.

"Yes," he answered. "It should go away over time if we can help you to discover what shocked you so much. It may have been something in your childhood long ago, or maybe something that happened in Paris. But once we get to the root of it by talking about your past, it should stop. Of course, it may take some time. It's hard to know how long."

"Depersonalization disorder?" I said. "Is that what you said it's called?"

He nodded.

"Do other people really experience this same exact thing?"

"Yes," he responded. "It's quite common, in fact."

"Common," I repeated, shaking my head. "It's common to feel like you have no personal identity?"

"It's just uncommon that it's gone on for so long without ever stopping," he responded. "But people feel this in short spells quite frequently. I would also like to have you try some anti-anxiety medication to see if it might alleviate some of the symptoms."

I shook my head. "No thanks. I really don't like medication. My mother has been taking antidepressants for years, and I don't like the whole idea of them—especially the way she regards her psychiatrist as some sort of god for having prescribed them."

"Fair enough," he said, smiling. "We wouldn't want that to happen, would we?"

Carl and I launched into our pursuit of the "cure" for the experience of no-self. I would drive to his office once a week and talk about my childhood, my relationships, and my interest in studying psychology. Maybe I was going to find some answers. Maybe the torturous fear would finally go away. Maybe my "I" would really come back if I discovered the underlying reason for its having left.

Inspired by Carl's complete trust in the healing power of the therapeutic process, I started looking seriously into psychology graduate programs. In the fall of 1986 I enrolled at John F. Kennedy University and began taking classes in their clinical psychology masters program. Carl reminded me often that he had confidence that "I" would return; it was only a matter of time. We both regarded our goal in therapy to be the return of the "I-ness," an endeavor we pursued together wholeheartedly.

After I had been seeing Carl for about three

months, I noticed a distinct change in his manner toward me. He started talking more frequently about himself, dropping small tidbits of information about his desire to have children and his purchase of a new home in the Santa Cruz mountains. When I would follow up on his statements with further questions, he would respond openly, and our discussions began to take on a decidedly personal flavor. He brought pictures of his new home and his dog to show me, sitting next to me on the couch as we looked at them together.

I was pleased with Carl's attention. He was the first person from whom I had received any modicum of hope, the first one who had made any definite statement about what he thought my experience meant. Although I realized the experience had been pathologized when he had labeled it depersonalization disorder, it didn't seem to matter since he thought the prognosis was so good. At least I had a name for the problem. And Carl would help to make it go away. His growing interest in me simply increased the hope that I wasn't going to be permanently stuck in the emptiness of "I." It also meant that I wasn't hopelessly crazy; otherwise, this obviously sane, personable man wouldn't be showing all the signs of becoming utterly infatuated with me.

Five months from the start of therapy, Carl ended our therapeutic relationship. He said that he wanted to continue to get to know me in other ways and that he could no longer be my therapist. We embarked on a romantic relationship, and he was soon a regular weekend visitor at my home in San Francisco. He began introducing me to his friends, careful to disguise how we had met and inventing various stories until he settled on telling them we had been introduced through mutual friends. Soon we were spending every weekend together, either in San Francisco or in Los Gatos, and talking to each other every evening on the phone during the week.

As I got to know Carl, I realized that he did not have the same enthusiasm for talking things out in our relationship as he had in our therapy. As often as not, he would tell me he had already "given at the office" and wasn't interested in discussing issues that might arise between us. He also assumed that my experience of no-self had somehow disappeared. He may even have intimated that I had really needed him to be my romantic partner in order to get my "self" back. And because I still believed that my experience was a problem that had to be hidden, I no longer discussed it with him.

After six months my relationship with Carl finally ended when I told him I was returning to therapy.

"Why?" he said. "I thought you were cured of your problems."

"Carl," I responded, "you won't talk to me about anything anymore. You think everything is fine, but it isn't. I still don't experience an 'I,' and I have to find some help in understanding what that means. There's still an incredible amount of fear."

"You mean that experience never stopped?"

"Never. There is not a single moment when the sense of being an individual person with a personal identity returns. It's been five years now. Maybe it's hopeless..."

"Here I thought you were feeling better," he said. "But you know, depersonalization disorder comes and goes over time. In some cases it never really goes away."

"Carl," I retorted, "this so-called depersonalization disorder has never come and gone. Don't you get that? Five years ago it started, in a moment, and it's never changed or gone away, even when I'm asleep!"

"I don't know what else it could be but symptoms of depersonalization," he replied. "Maybe you're just getting overly dramatic about the whole thing. I mean, you've been saying for a long time that you don't exist as an individual person, but here you are right in front of me talking to me. You're here, you know. You just think you're not."

"Why does everyone say the same thing? Do you think I'm just making the whole thing up? The fact that you see a body in front of you and hear a mouth speaking words doesn't mean a thing. The fact is, in my experience there is no person. It isn't something you can see from the outside. I've been telling you this for almost a year now!"

Carl's face hardened. He stopped the discussion with a wave of his hand and told me he was going for a walk. When he returned to his house, I was loading my bags and my daughter into the car. He stood in the driveway as I backed up and waved as we turned onto the road heading toward San Francisco. That was the last I saw of him.

In the weeks after leaving Carl, the fear grew stronger, turning my mind into a battleground where the emptiness of self appeared to be the enemy army. The emptiness deepened considerably as the fear waged its battle against it and would not remain in the background no matter how much the mind engaged in its various pursuits. I attempted to pour my attention into my classwork at John F. Kennedy University, plunging into an interesting academic life that kept the mind occupied reading new books, memorizing psychological theories, and writing papers. The emptiness rode along with every moment of attention, always present, never changing, like an uninvited guest that one is forced to accommodate.

Remembering Carl's diagnosis, I spent extra time reading up on the "dissociative disorders," including depersonalization, derealization, and dissociation. Clearly, certain characteristics of those disorders were or had been present in my experience, although none of them described the most prominent feature—the absolute absence of personal "I-ness" accompanied by unimpaired (and even improved) functioning in the world.

What did it mean that no answers were to be found in the psychological texts? Nearly six years of no-self and I was still no closer to finding anyone who even knew what it meant. I had fleeting memories of my friend Alan's statement, "People spend years in caves trying to have this experience." If the psychological literature didn't have anything to say about it, could it actually be a spiritual experience? But the mind still rejected this possibility. There was no bliss, no joy, no happiness at all. And it was so empty. But why had Alan reassured me, even after I had told him how horrible the whole thing was? Maybe I should at least find someone who knew something about spiritual experiences. There didn't appear to be anywhere else to go.

At this point I wasn't ready to venture too far from the psychological realm, so I tried therapy once more. This time, however, I chose a therapist who held degrees in both transpersonal and clinical psychology. He appeared to possess the perfect blend of training to solve the dilemma of whether I was encountering a pathological or a spiritual state. His ad in the local transpersonal journal was eloquently written, indicating a familiarity with spiritual experiences as well as a desire to compassionately accompany others through whatever struggles they were encountering.

I arrived late for our first appointment after taking the wrong freeway exit and breathlessly followed Sam Goldfarb into his house, which was located in a quiet neighborhood in the Richmond hills. He led me to a room in the back that he used as his office, and I plunged into my story, telling him in as much detail as possible about the emptiness, the lack of self, and the fear.

"Well," he said, "it seems to me you are either encountering a dramatic seventh chakra opening, a profound spiritual experience, or you're in a dissociative state in which you're fleeing from reality."

"That doesn't tell me much," I responded, "unless you know how to tell the difference between those two states."

"Well, it's not that easy to tell the difference," he said. "I guess we'll just have to start working together and see if it becomes obvious one way or the other."

I spent three years in therapy with Sam analyzing and unearthing childhood memories and feelings. Early in treatment Sam discarded the possibility that the experience might be a spiritual one, and we proceeded with the (unspoken) assumption that no-self was a state I had entered, in Sam's words, "to escape feeling fear, sadness, or other difficult emotions." It was, in other words, a defense mechanism, a psychological strategy for survival. Sam maintained that I had not received sufficient "mirroring" as a child, and the wounds that had developed by "not being seen" by others when I was young were now manifesting as this emptiness. He said I was narcissistically injured and had this "huge hole" inside me that I was trying but would never be able to fill.

Sam pushed me to express my pain by yelling, sobbing, and hitting pillows. He told me that the pain kept instigating my flight into emptiness because I was unwilling to face it fully, and until I faced it without running away, I wouldn't be healed.

Emptiness of self was again pathologized, which by no means changed the experience, but simply increased the fear of it. There were days when I could not even leave my house because my body was literally shaking with terror. My talks with Sam led the mind to believe that my problem was much more serious than I had ever imagined.

"The fear is getting worse, Sam," I cried, week after week.

"What are you so afraid of?" he asked, in his softest, most compassionate voice.

"I'm afraid of going crazy, of not being able to function at all, of not being able to take care of my daughter. I can hardly stand the fear anymore." Tears were pouring down my face.

"Go ahead and try to go crazy," he said. "Go on. I'll be here to pull you back."

"Sure," I yelled at him, "you'll be here. But so what? I'm totally terrified, and you're telling me I should jump right into it and you'll rescue me? I think what's happening is that you don't have a clue about what's really going on here, and you don't know what else to try. Maybe you should just be honest and admit you don't know, rather than making me more afraid than I was before."

"You know, Suzanne," he retorted, "you've been extremely difficult these last few months. You're always angry with me; I feel like I can't do anything right. I'd like to read you my notes about our last session. Would that be all right? I want you to know how I'm seeing all this anger you're directing toward me."

"You want to read me your notes?" I asked, incredulous. "Why do you want to do that?"

"I want you to know my impressions, my thoughts about what you're going through."

"Sure," I said, still puzzled. "Go ahead and read them if you really want to."

"OK, here goes." He flipped through his spiral notebook for a minute until he located the correct page. Then he took a deep breath and began reading. "'She's been devaluing me for several months now because I won't gratify her need to feel special. She used to see me as the 'good breast,' the nurturing object who was all-good, perfect, worthy of emulation. Now she sees me as the 'bad breast,' the all-bad, fallen-from-grace, deeply disappointing, frustrating, non-fulfilling object. Her pre-Oedipal wounding is more and more apparent, and her primitive defense mechanisms are operating full force. She's splitting, seeing me as the all-bad punisher. She's infuriated that I won't love her as the special one in my life.'"

I stared at Sam with my mouth open for several moments in utter disbelief, unable to speak. Was this how he had been seeing me for the past three years? All the time I'd been talking to him about the terror, the confusion, the difficulty of experiencing the cessation of personal identity, had he really interpreted it as a sign of object-relational splitting and borderline personality disorder?

I looked into Sam's eyes. He seemed calm, happy even, a smile curling the corners of his mouth as he gazed peacefully at me. He was proud of his analysis and proud to have shared it with me. He waited for my response for several minutes, and then, when none was forthcoming, he closed his eyes and leaned back in his chair. I was still speechless; the mind had been shocked into silence. I was still staring at him as I rose to my feet, gathered my jacket and purse, and started slowly for the door. Sam opened his eyes as I stood to leave. He looked at the clock, which showed a half hour remaining in the session, then turned a puzzled look in my direction.

"We aren't finished," he said. "Where are you going?"

"I'm leaving," I responded, hardly able to form the words. "I have nothing more to say. I can't believe I really heard what you just read. I..."

There was no more to say. I left his office in a fog, shaking off his insistent pleas for more talk. What more was there to say? He had made it clear that he interpreted the experience of no-self to be a sign of pathology, of deep wounding in the early stages of life for which the prognosis was poor. This

was the same voice that spoke through my fears—
the icy, reverberating voice of terror that circulated
in the mind, piercing any moments of peace or con-
tentment like a sharpened blade.

⟶

While I was in therapy with Sam, I became
involved in a relationship with a man I had met during one of my classes at JFK. As it turned out, he
had been a good friend of Sam's for many years.
Steve and I came together in the context of a psychological perspective. We spoke about psychological material, theoretical models, and relationship
issues in ways that constructed a bond of life pursuits. And we agreed that the intense fear that was
constantly coursing through my life, which I
described to him at regular intervals, was a sign of
some deeper psychological problem.

Since both of us were training to be psychotherapists, we adopted a psychological view of everything
that arose between us. We analyzed and interpreted
behaviors, we talked regularly about the symbolic
meanings of things, and we learned each other's
family histories in order to understand the deeper
"patterns" or "issues" that influenced our relationship. Like Claude, Steve had difficulty understanding what I meant when I said there was no "me." As
far as he was concerned, he was relating to a woman
who had every appearance of being someone.

Within the mysterious workings of the emptiness, the relationship with Steve developed and continued for nine years. Yet staying together didn't

occur for any identifiable reasons, and the relationship itself never brought back a reference point, even though the appearance of being someone was pursued by the mind. Because we came together in fear, the mind felt compelled to make the act of relating appear to be personal by constructing from memory what it thought it looked like to be a woman in relationship. Never for a moment in all those nine years, however, did Steve and I have a personal relationship, since there was never a "me" for him to be in relationship with.

From the occurrence of the emptiness of individual self in the spring of 1982 until the end of my therapy with Sam, I had consulted with ten psychotherapists. Although none of those therapies had done anything but substantiate the fears, I still believed there were no other socially sanctioned places to turn for help in understanding what had happened. So, after Sam, I sought out yet another therapist.

Lauren Spock was a clinical psychologist in her early fifties who had a solid reputation in the transpersonal community as both a therapist and a spiritual teacher. After listening to the description of my experience, she told me I should never go into the emptiness; it was simply too dangerous. What she meant by dangerous I will never know, because once those words were uttered, the fear became so enormous that it was impossible to ask for clarification. She further warned that I should never listen to anyone who recommended I go into the empti-

ness, because that very recommendation would sig-
nify they knew nothing about it. She said that she
was worried about me, and that I would soon be
unable to function if I kept going as I was.

During the three months I saw Lauren, I became
more and more terrified about what had happened to
me. When she left for her annual summer sojourn in
New York, we continued our therapy by telephone.
During the third phone session, she told me I was so
unstable she couldn't be responsible for me at a distance. She had decided to end our therapy, and she
gave me the name of another therapist who lived
close by. She asked me to leave a message on her
answering machine to let her know I had found someone else to work with.

Despite the fear, something always knew that
Lauren was wrong. It was the same something that
knew that all the therapists who had sided with the
voice of fear had been wrong. It seemed foolish to
seek out yet another therapist who was likely to
hold the same perspective, so I tried a new
approach. I found a traditional, psychodynamically
oriented psychologist, a woman who taught at some
of the local graduate schools, and started therapy
with her. The new approach consisted of not telling
her anything about the experience of no-self. Needless to say, the therapy was useless. She never knew
what I really needed to talk about, and I never trusted her ability to see my experience from a non-
pathologizing perspective. I spent one year in
therapy with her, talking about graduate school and
relationships and psychological theories. When it
was obvious I was never going to tell her my real
concerns, I quit.

Several months later, I tried a therapist recommended to me by a friend. She had been seeing David Kaye for years, and she trusted him implicitly. He was outspoken, upfront, and confrontational, and he concluded, a month into our therapy, that if I didn't know who I was I had no business becoming a therapist. He thought the experience of emptiness meant that I was having a psychotic experience and that I needed to have twice-weekly therapy to help me "work through" all the "pain I was repressing." Ten minutes into our sixth session, when he told me he felt that whatever he did was never enough for me, I stood up, told him I was quitting, and left.

My final experience with psychotherapy didn't even get to a first session. I had been asking around for therapists who had come through their own personal experiences of depersonalization. It seemed that if I was going to continue searching within the psychological context, I might as well call the experience by a clinical name in the hope that someone in that world would recognize it. I was put into contact with a woman who told me she couldn't see me because her practice was full. She asked if I wanted the names of other therapists I might call.

"That's OK," I declined, "I don't think so. What I really feel is that no one can help me."

"What an awful way to feel," she responded.

"Well, it just seems like after all these years in therapy, after seeing twelve different therapists, either I'm totally beyond help or I should give up on therapy altogether."

"Let me know if you change your mind," she said. "I might have an opening in a few months."

When I finished therapy with Sam, I was already in the second year of a doctoral program in psychology. In the fall of 1987 I had transferred to The Wright Institute after spending a year at JFK because I wanted to get a Ph.D. instead of a masters degree. All the subsequent experiences in therapy took me through the end of my graduate training.

The Wright Institute was a traditional, psychodynamically oriented psychology program, and most of the faculty and supervisors associated with the school held a rigorously analytic theoretical orientation. I was being trained to practice psychotherapy according to the Freudian "blank screen" model, in which the therapist says as little as possible while simultaneously attempting to come up with brilliant analytic interventions that will dramatically change their patients' lives.

We were encouraged to "work in the transference" and "pay attention to our countertransference" in order to use this material in the therapeutic process, since everything in therapy "happened in the relationship" between patient and therapist. We were repeatedly cautioned never to "gratify patients," which seemed to mean everything from not telling them how old we were or how we were feeling if they asked, to not giving them more than a cursory handshake after a particularly difficult session or even at the close of years of therapy.

The analytic stance felt like a straitjacket, and it was difficult to understand how it might be useful to patients, who in many cases ended up feeling worse about themselves than when they started therapy. I never took this stance toward any of the clients I saw through the Wright Institute training program, although I never mentioned this to my supervisors. I simply could not rebuff the natural human gestures of my clients, or turn those gestures back on them, or meet their inquiries with silence.

The analytic position delineates that if clients have positive feelings about the therapist, they are told that this is transference that needs to be worked through. If they have negative feelings about the therapist, they are told that this too is transference that needs to be worked through. If the therapist feels something about the patient, it's either countertransference or projective identification, a defense mechanism in which the patient projects repressed feelings onto the therapist and makes the therapist feel them instead.

I could never understand why someone would want to pay good money to a person who says little to them, refuses to respond to the simplest of questions, sees in their actions hidden, negative motivations ("the fact that you're two minutes late for therapy means that you're resistant to treatment"), and pathologizes their experience by interpreting everything they do as a sign of some deeper, underlying problem. Traditional psychotherapy seems to be based on a primordial fear of mystery, and this fear creates the tendency to reduce, interpret, or pathologize all manifestations of consciousness that do not fit the cultural norm.

Although I am well aware that not all therapists work in this manner, this was the model in which my training took place. It was equally disturbing to hear what analytically oriented psychotherapists said about their patients amongst themselves. I rarely heard expressions of compassion, sympathy, or even human understanding. Instead, each patient had a label according to their diagnosis. "You won't believe what my borderline patient did yesterday." Or, "The obsessive-compulsive I see at 10 o'clock is driving me crazy."

As I neared the end of my training, it became clear that I was looking in the wrong place to understand the experience of no-self, since, psychologically speaking, this experience was something of which I needed to be cured. The notion of "cure" involves trying to eliminate, stop, or change something that you, or more importantly your therapist, cannot accept as appropriate. But there was obviously no way the experience of individual identity was going to return, and it was now appallingly clear that the field of psychology hadn't the slightest clue about what was going on. Nevertheless, I finished the doctoral program and obtained licensure as a psychologist because it was just the next obvious thing to be done. I couldn't have explained why I was doing it. I never proceeded according to reasoning arrived at through the mind.

Of course, the fear was still pumping out its own brand of logic, which reasoned that I had to pursue a career as a psychologist because I needed to assume the appearance of being someone. Knowing you are no one doesn't fit the cultural model. In this world, emptiness is not an acceptable goal. Years later, my brother would make me laugh when he commented that I was the only one in our family to "make something of myself." The mind had apparently succeeded in its efforts to make me appear to be a person like everybody else.

7.

EMPTINESS RECOGNIZED AS VASTNESS

For the listener who listens in the snow
And, nothing himself, beholds
Nothing that is not there
And the nothing that is.
> —*Wallace Stevens*

A decade had passed since the personal reference point had disappeared, a decade spent searching for understanding while tormented by fear. No matter how much fear was experienced, however, the emptiness never fluctuated for a moment. I had looked to those who were considered the wise of our culture, those educated souls whose intellects had been developed through the rigors of academic training. Those "teachers of the postmodern age," known as psychotherapists, had tried their best to provide me with some understanding of the experience I had described to them. They had attempted to find words to explain something they did not understand.

Although well-meaning, all the therapists I spoke with were imprisoned by their ideas about how life should be interpreted and were unable to stay open to the possibility that reality could be experienced in many different ways. In the end, no one was willing to admit they simply didn't know.

In the spring of 1992, one year after finishing graduate school, I began to seek a spiritual perspective on the emptiness of personal self. I read voraciously, prowling bookstores endlessly for anything that might shed light on my experience. These efforts paid off handsomely when I discovered Buddhism. There were entire volumes written about *anatta* (no-self) and *shunyata* (emptiness), page after page devoted to describing, discussing, and investigating the experience I had lived with for the past ten years.

I read everything I could find. It was amazing that I had never discovered any of this material before. I was particularly struck by the following passage by the Dalai Lama: "Selflessness (no-self) is not a case of something that existed in the past becoming nonexistent. Rather, this sort of 'self' is something that never did exist."

In Buddhist circles, I learned, one is not met with stares of confusion and horror when describing no-self. In fact, I was getting the impression that not only was my experience considered a positive one, it was seen as the goal of every person who embarked on the Buddhist path.

One aspect of my experience that Buddhism was particularly helpful in explaining was that although individual identity had dropped away, all the personality functions remained completely intact. Now, however, those functions floated in a vastness that referred to no one. All the same experiences still happened, there just wasn't a "me" to whom they were happening. And the appropriate responses just happened as well, arising out of and then subsiding into themselves. Everything appeared and disappeared on the broad screen of the infinite—interactions, emotions, talk, actions of all kinds.

Without an individual self to direct action and speech, the concept of service took on an entirely new dimension. Now action and speech were seen to arise not out of any personal purpose, but out of what was needed in the moment for the situation at hand. There was no personal functioning, yet functioning in its entirety continued unimpaired—a co-presence of functioning and not-functioning, existing and not-existing.

The Buddhist texts explained this by saying that what remains in the state of no-self are empty functions (empty, that is, of individual personhood) called *skandhas*, or "aggregates." What speaks, then, is the speaking function, what thinks is the thinking function, what mothers is the mothering function, what feels is the feeling function, and so forth. These functions do the job of living in the world, and they are empty of individual self.

The five skandhas are generally translated as form; feelings and sensations; perceptions; mental formations; and consciousness. All experiences associated with the sense of self, according to the Buddhist teachings, can be analyzed into these five skandhas. There is no persisting self to be found over and above their functioning. These five "aggregates" do not in any way constitute a self. Rather, their interaction creates the illusion of self.

The worst fear we encounter as human beings is

the fear of annihilation. What happens, then, when annihilation occurs and still something remains? The Buddhists say that we have then stepped into truth. The skandhas remain but their truth (which is that they are empty) is revealed. This was my direct experience. But why had no one ever mentioned how bizarre and frightening the "step into truth" can be?

I still had not found any written descriptions of the transition or adjustment period that occurs when the self-consciousness abruptly disappears. Perhaps it was unusual for the experience to be so dramatic and abrupt; perhaps others had experienced a more gradual drop into emptiness and therefore not encountered the same extreme terror. It seemed improbable, however, that any true encounter with emptiness would not include at least some fear. The reality of the infinite must inevitably be terrifying to the flimsy illusion of the finite self. How could it not be? And why hadn't anyone discussed it?

A closer look at the language and assumptions of modern-day spirituality provided some possible answers to these questions. There are widely shared, unquestioned notions in spiritual circles about what constitutes a true spiritual experience—notions that are undisputed primarily because they form a closed system. If you dispute their validity, the system insinuates, you must not be having the true experience, and therefore you have no basis on which to dispute.

Fearlessness is regarded as one of the signs of a valid spiritual awakening. Along with infinite love, bliss, joy, and ecstasy, fearlessness is considered one of the indisputable markers of an enlightened life. People have always looked for things they can navigate by, signs that point the way and tell them when they have arrived at their destination. The interpretations of spiritual experiences have been managed or organized by this need to navigate and have thereby lost their validity.

We have become convinced that the presence of particular thoughts, feelings, or actions is the only way we can really know if someone is enlightened. The checklist of enlightened attributes is both lengthy and complex. Is this really love, we ask, in the presence of a supposedly enlightened being? Or bliss? Do they still have thoughts, we want to know, since we have heard that a mind empty of thoughts is surely a sign of spiritual advancement? And what is this? Is fear present? Well, the presence of fear proves they couldn't possibly be having a true spiritual experience. In fact, however, the presence of fear means only that fear is present, and nothing more.

At this point, an old friend from my TM days called, and I talked to him about my experience. He reminded me of something Maharishi Mahesh Yogi had said a long time ago. Evidently Maharishi had made it clear that Cosmic Consciousness (the first stage of awakening) was a horrible experience and that the guru's presence was essential to help the person move quickly through the stage of witness awareness. Without the guru, Maharishi claimed, the person could be lost indefinitely in confusion and fear. The guru did not actually give someone the experience of enlightenment, he said. Rather, the guru verified such an experience by saying, "Yes, that's it!"

My friend also reminded me that Maharishi had said the same thing about God Consciousness—not that it was as disturbing an experience as Cosmic Consciousness, but that the guru was needed to verify the state so the next stage of consciousness could reveal itself.

───

One of the books I read in my search through the spiritual literature was a compilation of interviews with a variety of contemporary spiritual teachers entitled *Timeless Visions, Healing Voices*. The book was written by Stephan Bodian, a therapist in Marin County who also edited a well-known spiritual magazine. One of the interviews in particular, with a teacher named Jean Klein, seemed to describe my experience precisely, and I made an appointment to talk with Stephan, although not without trepidation, given my past experiences with therapists.

Stephan had a calm, quiet presence, and I found him surprisingly easy to talk to. I described the experience of emptiness as completely as I could, mentioning the tremendous fear and anxiety. He asked me several clarifying questions and then said something I had never expected to hear from a psychotherapist: "You seem to have experienced a profound spiritual awakening. This appears to be the state of freedom that all the spiritual traditions, particularly the advaita (nondual) tradition, describe. This is wonderful!"

When I asked why he thought I was experiencing

so much fear, he said he did not know, but he recommended that I talk with his teacher, Jean Klein, who happened to be coming to Berkeley the following week to give some talks. Jean, he said, taught in the tradition of Ramana Maharshi and other great advaita sages that the individual self is simply a fabrication of the mind, and that the real Self is a nonpersonal, all-inclusive awareness.

About ten days later I joined a group of about sixty people at a community center in north Berkeley to await the appearance of Jean Klein. He entered the room from a side door and walked slowly to his chair in the front of the room. He was a slender man, elderly and frail, with a kind face and sparkling eyes. He sat down and closed his eyes, sinking everyone into silent meditation. He remained in the silence for at least fifteen minutes, then slowly opened his eyes and began speaking. His voice was heavily accented, and everyone leaned slightly forward to catch each word. He talked briefly about freedom of awareness, making several suggestions to his students about perceiving without projections. He then asked for questions. I stood up and asked if I could have his comments on an experience I had been having for the past ten years.

"Ten years ago, quite abruptly, my sense of being an individual self dissolved, stopped, turned off," I began. "Ever since then I have never felt like there's an 'I' there anymore. When I drive a car or speak these words or walk down the street, there is never an experience of a person who is doing these things. No person is there anymore."

"You mean there is no experience of a 'me'?" Jean asked.

"That's right," I answered, "there's no 'me.' There used to be one, but now there isn't anymore."

"Well, that's perfect," Jean replied. "Perfect."

"But Jean, why is there so much anxiety? And why is there no joy?"

"You must stop the part of the mind that constantly keeps trying to look back at the experience," he responded. "Get that part out of the way, then joy will come."

No one else in the room could possibly have known how appropriate his words were. There was a part of the mind—perhaps what we call the self-reflective or introspective function—that kept turning to look and, finding emptiness, kept sending the message that something was wrong. It was a reflex that had developed during the years of living in the illusion of individuality, a reflex we commonly consider necessary to know ourselves. We "look within" repeatedly to determine what we think and feel, to make a study of ourselves and track our states of mind and heart. Now that there was no longer an "in" to look "into," the self-reflective reflex was adrift, but it persisted. It kept turning in and turning in, unable to come to terms with the fact that there was no "in" anymore, only emptiness. What Jean taught me that evening was crucial, and I am forever grateful to him.

After his talk, Jean extended an invitation through one of his students to meet with him privately the following week. I drove to Marin County and found him sitting in the garden next to the house where he was staying. He greeted me as I approached and motioned me to sit next to him. He asked me to tell him the whole story of the change of consciousness, while he listened carefully, smiling sweetly and nodding his head as I spoke. He then made a few comments about how I was perceiving purely, freshly, out of the immediacy of what is.

We talked for about forty-five minutes, then he inquired about my health. I told him my health was excellent, and he responded that he was glad. We sat side by side in silence for another fifteen minutes before I rose to leave. He shook my hand and said how happy he was to know that I was living in the "knowing."

After meeting with Jean, I began contacting other spiritual teachers whose books or articles made mention of the emptiness of personal self. I wrote to a handful of the best-known Buddhist and Hindu teachers, describing my experience in detail and asking for their comments. From all of them I received wonderful, interesting letters filled with praise and excitement. Each in their own way made it clear that what had happened was wonderful. Each letter verified the experience as the realization of the true nature of all creation.

A profound relief accompanied the reading of each one. But the experience itself still brought no joy, and fear was still present. How could that be? I corresponded and met with several teachers to solicit their response to this one central question: If what I am experiencing is a true awakening, then where is the joy, and why is fear still arising?

Christopher Titmuss, an English teacher of Buddhist vipassana meditation, told me how significant it was to realize the insubstantiality of the "I." Addressing my fear that the experience meant that I was insane, he wrote, "In spiritual language, insanity is the absence of such experiences as yours, since it (the absence) renders absolute authority to the 'me, me, me' culture. The madness of the belief of that culture has personal, social, and global consequences."

He said that he thought the reason there was an absence of joy or deep appreciation of the experience was that I didn't understand it. "How could you?" he wrote. "You have no previous reference for it. How can 'I' understand 'not I?'" He recommended that I find someone locally who I felt "understands my experience, has had such experiences, and who knows the value and joy of realizing the emptiness of 'I.'"

In further discussions held when he was in northern California to lead a summer retreat, Christopher described how the calm acceptance of the experience would inevitably bring a quieting of any movement in the thoughts and feelings that gave rise to fear.

"You need to be reassured," he said. I could feel the quiet integrity behind his words. "The reassurance will allow a quieting of the fear. Out of the quieting will arise the bounty of the experience and a deepening of insight."

He continued, "When someone comes to me and tells me they have realized the emptiness, I usually tell them, 'Come back in a year and a day, and let's see where you are then.' If they can say the same thing to me then and if their lives have been profoundly affected, then I'll say, 'OK, that's it.'"

"Is twelve years enough?" I asked.

"I would say you were eminently qualified—overqualified even," he responded, and we both laughed heartily.

Without question, what I had lacked during the entire twelve-year journey was calm acceptance. For twelve years I had received no reassurance; I had been completely alone. The mind did not know what to make of it all, and it searched constantly for understanding and meaning. It took close to eleven years to finally accept that the mind was simply incapable of grasping the vastness of the experience of no personal self. This acceptance cleared the way for the mind to comprehend that an ungraspable experience is just that. It's neither wrong nor crazy—it's simply ungraspable.

"Why don't we go into my office. We can talk there," said Reb Anderson, the abbot of Green Gulch Zen Center, located on coastal farmland just north of the Golden Gate Bridge. I followed him up the stone pathway set into the steep hillside, past the small wooden building that served as office and bookstore for the Zen community, and stepped out onto a wide expanse of lawn dotted with huge eucalyptus trees and colorful flower beds. We sat on a low wooden bench in the autumn sunlight. "Nice office," I remarked. He smiled and then fixed me with his solid, intense gaze. I told him my story and asked him his opinion about why I wasn't finding any joy in the experience.

"The experience of emptiness of self *is* bliss," he said. "The emptiness knowing itself is bliss, but it's a bliss that is not the same as relative bliss. It's obvious to me that you are completely in bliss at this very moment."

He went on to explain that the relative mechanisms of the skandhas cannot perceive the bliss of emptiness, and therefore it made sense that the bliss that was occurring was hard to recognize. Reb's description loosened a rigidity in the way the mind had been interpreting the experience.

Jack Kornfield, vipassana teacher and cofounder of the Spirit Rock Meditation Center in Marin County, and Ram Dass, well-known author, lecturer, and disciple of Neem Karoli Baba, also sent helpful, encouraging words, both doing his best to provide reassurance and accompaniment. Both of them reminded me that it takes years to grow into and integrate such a profound shift in consciousness. In a phone conversation, Jack said, "This is a wonderful experience. There's nothing to be afraid of...In the East the word *akinchina* is used to describe a person who is fully awakened. It's translated to mean one who has nothing, longs for nothing, stands upon nothing, and becomes nothing."

Ram Dass said that you have "done remarkably well with this, in being able to develop and maintain the life you have with family and practice, which shows incredible strength." He also told me that we "share no-self together, along with Maharaji," and that there is a Tibetan great wish that one says in honoring one's guru: "May your wisdom mind and mine remain inseparable. Wisdom mind," said Ram Dass, "is the place of no-self."

Hameed Ali (A. H. Almaas), a spiritually oriented psychologist and author, responded to my letter as follows: "I recognize your experience as something real, as a spiritual awakening. It is definitely not pathological, and it makes sense that many people will not understand it. I have had similar awakenings as part of an ongoing process and hence find your descriptions familiar.

"The way it happened to you is different from how my process of awakening occurred, and from the way I teach in my work. And the fact that your experience goes through stages and developments is also real and corresponds to how the process of awakening happens to many individuals. I believe your childhood experiences have prepared you for it, and the meditation and retreats you did also contributed. The fear and terror you mention is usual under such conditions, and it requires a great deal of understanding to see through it and go beyond it. It seems you have done well on your own without the guidance of a teacher."

But the clearest acknowledgment I received of my experience was from a spiritual teacher who was no longer alive. When I "met" Ramana Maharshi through his dialogues with his disciples, I knew I had met my spiritual father. He described my experience in such a direct and simple fashion that it left absolutely no room for doubt about what I was encountering.

Ramana: After transcending the *dehatma buddhi* (I-am-the-body idea), one becomes a jnani. In the absence of that idea there can be neither doership nor doer. So the jnani performs no actions. That is his experience.

Question: I see you doing things. How can you say that you never perform actions?

Ramana: The radio sings and speaks, but if you

open it you will find no one inside. Similarly, my existence is like the space; though this body speaks like the radio, there is no one inside as a doer.

Question: I find this hard to understand. Could you please elaborate on this?

Ramana: The potter's wheel goes on turning round even after the potter has ceased to turn it. In the same way, the electric fan goes on revolving for some minutes after we switch off the current. The predestined karma which created the body will make it go through whatever activities it was meant for, and the jnani goes through all these activities without the notion that he is the doer of them—because he is not. It is hard to understand how this is possible, but the jnani knows and has no doubts.... He knows he is not the body, and he knows that he is not doing anything, even though his body may be engaged in some activity. These explanations are for the onlookers who think of the jnani as one with a body and cannot help identifying him with his body.

Question: It is said that the shock of realization is so great that the body cannot survive it.

Ramana: If a man must at once leave his body when he realizes the Self, I wonder how any knowledge of the Self or the state of realization can come down to others.... The fact is that any amount of action can be performed, and performed quite well, by the jnani without his identifying himself with it in any way or ever imagining that he is the doer. Some power acts through his body and uses his body to get the work done.

Question: You say the jnani sees no differences, yet it seems to me that he appreciates differences better than an ordinary man. If sugar is sweet and wormwood is bitter to me, he seems to realize it so. In fact, all forms, all sounds, all tastes, etc. are the same to him as they are to others. If so, how can it be said that these are mere appearances? Do they not form part of his life experience?

Ramana: I have said that equality is the true sign of a jnani. The very term equality implies the existence of differences. It is a unity that the jnani perceives in all differences, which I call equality. Equality does not mean ignorance of distinctions. When you have the realization, you can see that these differences are very superficial, that they are not substantial or permanent and what is essential in all these appearances is the one truth, the real. That I call unity.

Reading more and more of Ramana's words led me to an astounding passage. When asked by a disciple if it was necessary to be associated with the wise (*sat-sanga*) in order for the Self to be realized, Ramana answered: "Yes, [what is required is] association with the unmanifest *sat* or absolute existence.... The sastras say that one must serve (be associated with) the unmanifest *sat* for *twelve years* in order to attain Self-realization...but as very few can do that, they have to take second best, which is association with the manifest *sat*, that is, the Guru."

Poonjaji, a well-known and respected disciple of Ramana Maharshi, wrote that "in between the arrival of the bus and your waiting to board, there was the Void where there was no past and no future. This Void revealed itself to itself. This was due to your merits gained in many previous lifetimes. This is a wonderful experience. It had to stay eternally with you.... This is perfect freedom.... You have become liberation (*moksha*) of the realized sages."

Gangaji, a teacher in the lineage of Ramana Maharshi and Poonjaji, wrote back, clearly excited about what I had described to her. "I was thrilled to get your letter!" she said. "Of course we must meet. I am very, very happy that you have directly discovered yourself to be no individual 'I.' This realization of the inherent emptiness—which is pure consciousness—of all phenomena is true fulfillment. In the face of conditioned existence, much fear can be initially felt. Ultimately, the fear is also revealed to be only that same empty consciousness."

Andrew Cohen, a spiritual teacher who also studied with Poonjaji and wrote several books describing his experience of awakening to the awareness that there is no personal self, replied that he would love to meet with me to discuss the experience I had described in the letter. We spent several hours speaking about the emptiness of personal self. He conveyed how exciting it is to live in the awareness that there is not and never has been a personal reference point for anything.

I wrote him again to share how delightful our

talk had been and how the awareness of "being no one was starting to show itself as the awareness of the non-locatable mystery that had always been the doer behind everything." After my talk with Andrew I began seeing how the emptiness of a "me" was full of exquisite infinity. This awareness was to deepen and move to the foreground radically in the next month.

Andrew wrote back that he was "delighted to hear that our meeting had had a profound effect on your already awakened condition. I had felt the first time we spoke that you had more ideas about enlightenment than you were aware of. You are indeed a rare individual because in most cases when an individual has come as far as you have (which is rare in and of itself), they usually unknowingly take a position in their experience which makes it difficult if not impossible to proceed any farther. Your openness and receptivity is a sign of true humility, which alone makes all things possible."

In the summer of 1993, a friend told me about a Zen teacher he had been studying with for several years. Dharma heir of a well-known Western Buddhist roshi, this teacher, I was told, was a highly competent spiritual guide. He lived fairly close to my home, where he both taught Zen practice to a community of students and maintained a private practice in psychotherapy. From the first time I met Richard McGuire, I knew I had found an understanding friend.

After listening to my story, Richard told me that it seemed I was still in the winter of the experience and that the blossoms of springtime would bring the joy I sought. His description of spiritual development in terms of seasons was a reassuring and highly appropriate one. Seasons arise and dissolve with an ancient rhythm of their own. They are the work of the mystery, not constructed by an individual doer, rising one after the other in an eternal, dependable rotation. Spring always arrives. Always. Richard was assuring me that I was encountering just one season of the emptiness and that I could trust it to change, just as surely as the spring always arrives, even after the longest winter.

Richard was able to provide me with the solid context of a tradition that was intimately familiar with the emptiness of individual self. He told me Zen stories and anecdotes about ancient Chinese masters. He showed me how I was "seeing with the same eyes" as the ancestors. When he said I was having the most classic experience he'd ever encountered—straight from the ancient texts—I laughed and said, "And here I thought it was just insanity!"

"That's classic too," he responded.

In the end, Richard's greatest gift to me was the knowing that spring would arrive. And arrive it did.

A winter that lasts eleven years is a hard one to bear. Maharishi's statement that the guru is needed to say, "That's it!" indicates the extent to which being alone can leave one open to being overwhelmed by fear when the fear passes itself off for truth. The apparently personal aspects that still remain, even in the emptiness of a personal self, are constantly affected by fear. They still get stuck in their functioning, like a record stuck in a groove, when terror operates at such a high pitch. When they get stuck, the experience becomes fixed, clamped into place, and the seasons cannot follow their natural, easy cycle of unfolding.

I had gotten stuck in the emptiness—what Richard called the "Zen sickness"—and it had become a vicious circle. Afraid of what had happened, I had isolated myself out of fear, which then just created more fear and more isolation.

He also told me how unusual it was to transition into the emptiness so abruptly and completely. With others he had observed, the transition had occurred in a piecemeal fashion, with discrete openings over time that allowed interludes of acclimation. Because such an abrupt shift in consciousness is uncommon and thus lonely, it can lead to an increased level of fear until one can "catch up with the experience" and give it a context. The mind must learn that it can't grasp the experience of emptiness; in fact, it doesn't need to grasp it. But the mind doesn't take kindly to ungraspable experiences and tends to pathologize them simply because it can't understand them. Out of its own inability to understand, it sends the message that such experiences are wrong or crazy.

I continued to ask Richard why the fear kept arising. He took the traditional Buddhist view that the presence of fear meant that something was incomplete, and he started to suggest practices I might do to get rid of it. I responded by telling him that there was no one who could do any of those practices, since there was not a locatable doer to be the practitioner.

This period in our friendship became a turning point. By suggesting that I find some way to get rid of the fear, Richard was clearly operating on the presupposition that there was a personal doer who could accomplish this task. He was also implying that the presence of fear meant that something was wrong and needed to be eliminated. Apparently, he did not actually experience the emptiness of personal "I-ness." He was taking the presence of fear to mean there must be a personal reference point who was afraid. However, in the entire time I had been discussing the experience with him, I had insisted that the fear never referred to a someone.

I began to wonder aloud whether Richard shared the experience of knowing in a moment-to-moment way that there was no personal doer. Finally he admitted that, though he had given the impression that he did, he in fact did not. He was verifying my experience on the basis of his years of study of ancient texts and on glimpses into the emptiness of all phenomenon that had lasted minutes, days, or weeks.

Speaking with authority from the position of traditional Zen Buddhism, he had appeared to be more of an expert than he actually was. He couldn't help me with the fear because he didn't fully understand the emptiness. He had also been influenced by psychological theories as well as by the belief in Zen that one must do "character work" in order to evolve. When he began to tell me I needed to work on my character, I knew his advice was predicated on the assumption that there is an individual doer who can work on its character. I had realized that such a doer does not exist, so the idea of character work seemed absurd.

I reminded him that I experienced no "I" who could do inner work. As a matter of fact, there was no "inner" to work on. Once it was clear that Richard didn't share the experience I was describing to him, I thanked him for the accompaniment he had provided and took my leave.

8.

THE SECRET OF EMPTINESS

Midnight. No waves,
no wind, the empty boat
is flooded with moonlight.
　　　　　　—Dogen

I am not, but the Universe is Myself.
　　　　　　—Shih T'ou

Although I had received a great deal of reassurance from the people I had contacted about my experience, the wintertime of no-self was still not yielding much joy. As it turned out, the joy was to arrive all at once, crashing onto the shores of awareness suddenly and irrevocably, just as the first wave of the dropping away of self had occurred twelve years before.

From the clear experience of emptiness of self, my state of consciousness was about to transition abruptly into the next season—the experience that not only is there no personal self, there is also *no other*. In other words, I was about to shift permanently into unity awareness, in which the emptiness that dominated my consciousness was seen to be the very substance of all creation. Once the secret of emptiness was revealed in this way, I began to describe it as the "vastness."

In the midst of a particularly eventful week, I was driving north to meet some friends when I suddenly became aware that I was driving through myself. For years there had been no self at all, yet here on this road, everything was myself, and I was driving through me to arrive where I already was. In essence, I was going nowhere because I was everywhere already. The infinite emptiness I knew myself to be was now apparent as the *infinite substance* of everything I saw.

In the wake of this transition to the vastness of emptiness, I began to meditate intensively. I spent hours each morning and hours again each night just sitting in the vastness, as blossoms began appearing on the tree of emptiness. A strong pull arose to do a solitary retreat, so I arranged to stay for a long mid-January weekend at a Buddhist retreat center in the Santa Cruz mountains.

As I drove through the wintry landscape on my way there, everything seemed more fluid. The mountains, trees, rocks, birds, sky were all losing their differences. As I gazed about, what I saw first was how they were one; then, as a second wave of perception, I saw the distinctions. But the perception of the substance they were all made of did not occur through the physical body. Rather, the vastness was perceiving itself out of itself at every point in itself. A lovely calm pervaded everything—no ecstasy, no bliss, just calm.

At the same time, something else began emerging

which continues to this day—something I can only describe as a "thickening into unity" that was both experiential and perceptual. From that day forth I have had the constant experience of both moving through and being made of the "substance" of everything. This is what is experienced first—the stuff of unity, its texture, its flavor, its substance. This non-localized, infinite substance can be perceived not with the eyes or ears or nose, but by the substance itself, out of itself. When the substance of unity encounters itself, it knows itself through its own sense organ. Form is like a drawing in the sand of oneness, where the drawing, the sand, and the finger that draws it are all one.

On my own with the vastness, I had encountered the very insight that did the work of exposing the fear and releasing its hold. I realized that the mind had been clinging tenaciously to the erroneous notion that the presence of fear meant something about the validity of the experience of no-self. Fear had tricked the mind into taking its presence to mean something that it did not. Fear was present, yes, but that was it! The presence of fear in no way invalidated the experience that no personal self existed. It meant only that fear was present.

Fear didn't need to go anywhere for the personal self to be seen to be non-existent. After all, where could it possibly go? It had never existed. Nothing needed to change or be eradicated; nothing needed to do anything at all but to be. Everything occurs simultaneously—form and emptiness, pain and enlightenment, fear and awakening. Once seen, it seemed so incredibly simple.

Fear's grip now broke, and joy arose at once. The

experience of emptiness had given up its secret. The emptiness was seen to be nothing but the very substance of everything. I finally saw what had been in front of me the whole time but had been obscured by fear: There is not only no individual self, but also no other. No self, no other. Everything is made of the same substance of vastness.

Arriving at the retreat center in the late afternoon, I unloaded my bags at the cabin and went for a walk in the surrounding woods. I knew myself to be made of nothing and everything, just like all of creation. How could I have missed it before? It was right there in front of me the whole time, as close as the emptiness, as empty as the emptiness, and as full.

All the Zen stories Richard had told me came flooding back, and I began laughing and crying uproariously, unable to stop. Finally I fell to the ground, weak with the vision of it all. For twelve years I had known, seen, breathed emptiness, and now it extended throughout the universe in great tidal waves of empty fullness. That everything was unified in the emptiness now seemed like the most obvious thing in the world, but it had taken so long for me to stumble on it. I guess it had stumbled on itself.

Needless to say, nothing has ever been the same since. The fact that "I" no longer existed, that there was no person anymore, gave way finally and completely to the realization that there is nothing that is not myself. What remains when there is no self is all that is.

Maharishi's description of the three stages of awakening—Cosmic Consciousness, God Consciousness, and Unity Consciousness—now appeared to be incredibly relevant. The initial months of my experience, in which witness awareness persisted throughout waking, dreaming, and sleeping, was clearly the state of Cosmic Consciousness. Because of the abrupt and radical alteration of every previous manner of perception, this state of consciousness horrified the mind.

The dramatic shift to Unity Consciousness was also self-evident. When the substance of all creation is perceived first and distinctions second, there is no doubt what state of consciousness is prevailing.

However, I still found myself wondering what Maharishi had meant by God Consciousness. He had always described it as a state in which all of creation is perceived to be infused with the sacred, the divine. The perceiver is perceiving directly out of the awareness of God. Nothing I had ever experienced fit that particular description. Nor had I ever heard Maharishi describe anything resembling the experience, so clearly delineated by the Buddhists, that one is not an individual self.

It was not until I discovered a story about Shakespeare written by Jorge Luis Borges that I entertained the possibility that God consciousness was really the consciousness of being no one. "In him there was no one," the story begins, and goes on to explain that, when he was a child, Shakespeare thought that everyone knew they were no one as well. When he talked to his friends about the experience, however, he encountered blank looks, which "showed him his mistake and made him realize that an individual had best not differ from his species." The story describes a life lived in the wintertime of the emptiness, where the mind, juiced by fear, tried everything my mind had attempted to spark the return of a personal reference point. It searched for it in familiar people, intense emotional states, and sexual involvements, but never for a moment did those things refer to a someone.

When Shakespeare became an actor, the story goes on, he found the perfect profession, where he got to "play at being someone before an audience who played at taking him for that person." Although he spent his entire life attempting to reconstitute a sense of being someone, he never succeeded, though to everyone around him he certainly appeared to be someone.

The story concludes: "The tale runs that before or after death, when [Shakespeare] stood face to face with God, he said to Him, 'I, who in vain have been so many men, want to be one man—myself.' The voice of the Lord answered him out of the whirlwind, 'I too have no self; I dreamed the world as you dreamed your work, my Shakespeare, and among the shapes of my dreams are you, who, like me, are many men and no one.'"

According to this account, which admittedly is fictional, Shakespeare was constantly being seduced by fear into regarding the emptiness as wrong or problematic. He took the presence of fear to mean that the emptiness was a "strange ailment" and therefore spent his life trying to make it appear that he was someone. I know this experience well. The ten years that followed the abrupt awakening to no-self were spent trying to look like I was someone. The fear that fuels such a pursuit is relentless. The mind's contact with the unimaginable, ungraspable, unthinkable vastness sends it into a frenzy of terror, in which it insists that something must be horribly awry; otherwise, it argues, the terror would not be present. This is the wintertime of emptiness.

The final paragraph of the story declares that the consciousness of God is the realization of being no one. From the perspective of the infinite, it is obvious that the individual self absolutely does not exist. The idea that we have a self that controls, arbitrates, or is the doer behind our actions is absurd. The individual self is nothing but an idea of who we are. Ideas are ideas—and nothing more. An idea can never be the doer or creator of anything; it can only be what it is— an idea.

9.

LIVING THE VASTNESS

Out beyond ideas of
wrongdoing and rightdoing
there lies a field.
I'll meet you there.
When the soul lies down in that grass,
the world is too full to talk about.
Ideas, language, even the phrase each other
doesn't make any sense.
                    — *Rumi*

This life is now lived in a constant, ever-present awareness of the infinite vastness that I am. In this state, there is absolutely no reference point, yet an entire range of emotions, thoughts, actions, and responses are simultaneously present. The infinite— which is at once the substance of everything and the ocean within which everything arises and passes away—is aware of itself constantly, whether the mind and body are sleeping, dreaming, or waking.

In every moment, this body-mind circuitry is consciously participating in the sense organ through which the infinite perceives itself. There is never a locatable "me." In fact, the non-locatability of the vastness is the predominant flavor of the experience, and the infinity of this non-locatability is forever revealing itself to be more and more infinite.

At the bus stop in Paris, the "me" was annihilated, and it has never reappeared in any form. With this annihilation, there occurred the realization that a "me" has *never* existed who is the doer behind what has appeared to be "my" life. In recent years, it has also become clear that not only is there no "me," there is also no "other." The "no other-ness" is now so dominant that nothing else is perceived. Life is being lived out of the infinite substance of which it is made, and this substance—which is what and who we all are—is constantly aware of itself out of itself. What an extraordinary way to live!

The vastness never requires that something must go away for it to be the vastness. After all, where could anything go in this vastness? However, an entire range of "self-referential" emotions, such as embarrassment, self-consciousness, shame, envy, self-pity, self-reflection, and introspection, have simply ceased to arise. Since the individual self to which they referred no longer exists, they have nothing around which to form.

The same is true for the self-referencing aspect of all thoughts, body sensations, emotions, and actions. Although these experiences continue to occur, they no longer refer to a someone, a me. Nor do they arise anymore to serve a personal purpose or to achieve a goal. Thinking never precedes action or speech. Everything has an immediacy that is empty of personally directed intention. The presence of any thoughts, feelings, or actions is never interpreted to mean anything other than that they are present. The vastness perceives purely that thoughts are thoughts, feelings are feelings, actions are actions. There is no longer any wondering about whether a particular thought is right or wrong. In fact, no judgment about good or bad or right or wrong ever arises; everything is simply what it is.

In this state, nothing is ever experienced as a problem. To see anything as a problem, one would have to assume that something needs to change or go away for the problem to be solved. But I never relate to circumstances, experiences, or people as if they need to be anything other than what they are—because what they are is the infinite vastness. Nothing has to change, go away, or transform itself into something else for the vastness to be the vastness. The vastness is always who and what everything is.

Take, for example, the relationship to strong emotions like anger. The relationship of the vastness to anger is similar to the relationship of the ocean to the seaweed floating around in it. The ocean would never complain about the presence of seaweed and insist that it be removed for the ocean to be the ocean. In a similar manner, the vastness would never complain about the presence of anger or anything else that arises in it—and is simultaneously made of it—or insist that this arising cease. The vastness is never altered, no matter how numerous or intense the arisings. Nothing that occurs is ever regarded as a problem.

It is only quite recently that the vastness has begun to encounter itself directly in every person it meets. In the first decade of the experience, which I call the wintertime of the emptiness, there was tremendous fear that being no one was wrong. How can relationships exist, said the fear, if there is no one here relating? But exist they did, though they never referred to a someone, a me. The mind was totally confounded by the mystery of relationships occurring for a non-personal purpose and in the absence of a personal self. Over the years, however, the mind was forced to acknowledge that, despite its fears, ordinary functioning never diminished—whether in relating, mothering, working, studying, or paying the bills.

In the wintertime of relationships, there was a constant attempt to look like I was someone in relation to a person who took me to be that someone, even though I always knew I was no one. The memory of what it was like to be someone lingered, and the mind's fear about being no one inspired so much anxiety that relationships evoked a fear-constructed outline of somebodyness. Once it became clear that the presence of fear and anxiety meant only one thing—that they and everything else were present simultaneously in the vastness—then the relational season changed.

The springtime of relationships was awesome. To see with the eyes of the infinite—which is the substance of everything and perceives itself from within every particle of itself using its own sense organ—that relationships had also never involved a personal doer was so radical a vision that the mind "rolled over" and admitted that it simply could not grasp this inconceivable truth. Once the mind admitted to the parameters of its own sphere and stopped pathologizing what lay outside it, the non-personal, indescribably joyful flavor of the vastness experiencing itself moved radically to the foreground forever.

With the realization that everything was made of the same substance, relationships ceased to exist, since there was no longer any experience of an other. Without an other, there was simply nothing separate to be related to. Of course, the relational function continued as before, and it always looked like relationships were proceeding unimpaired.

What seems to have occurred at the bus stop in Paris is that the human circuitry of this life started to participate consciously in the sense organ with which the vastness is constantly perceiving itself. The vastness is the substance of all things, existing everywhere simultaneous with the appearance of form. Form exists simultaneously as that vastness and in that vastness, like a drawing in the sand in which the drawing itself is made of the same substance as what is "inside" and "outside" of it. In the same way, everything that appears to be form is not separate from the vastness.

The human circuitry is made of the same substance. When it consciously participates in the sense organ that the vastness is always using to perceive itself, the human circuitry becomes aware—not through its own sense organs, but through the sense organ of the vastness—that the substance of the infinite is its naturally occurring state. Seeing this, the circuitry joins the undulation of the vastness in a conscious way and begins to experience unceasing awe at everything that is.

As I have said before, when it becomes clear that there is no personal reference point, it also becomes apparent that there never was a personal reference point, and that everything is done and has always been done by an unseen doer. This doer doesn't start doing only when it is seen to be the doer. It has always been the doer; the personal self has never been the doer. Thus, life as usual continues to unfold; everything gets done, just as it did before the realization of the vastness occurred. Since there has never been a personal doer in any case, the realization of this truth does nothing to change how functioning occurs. All the functions continue as before—thinking, feeling, acting, relating. The difference is that it is now clear that they have never referred or belonged to a someone.

In the same way, the personal pronouns that appear in this book do not refer to a someone. There is no "me," no "I," no "mine." The descriptions that have been given are simply a flavor of the vastness, the infinite experiencing itself out of itself—there is absolutely no someone to whom these descriptions refer.

While the functions continue to function, it is now seen that they have always been engaged not for a personal purpose, but to do whatever the vastness deems obvious in the service of freedom. The vastness has its own non-personal desire to perceive itself directly through itself using the circuitry of every human being. This conscious participation by the circuitry in the sense organ of the vastness is the state of freedom—the naturally occurring human state. The mystery of the vastness knows within itself the most direct means to employ for that freedom to show itself. This circuitry is employed in a moment-to moment way in service to this mysterious vastness and always has been.

In relationships as well, all the functions continue as before, except that self-referencing thoughts, emotions, and sensations have ceased to arise. For example, sexuality still functions, but without the lust or longing that are the self-referencing aspects of that function. Sex serves no personal desire and has no deeper meaning that makes it anything but what it is at the moment. Like all the other functions, the sexual function is engaged when the vastness deems obvious, for a mysterious, non-personal purpose. When lovemaking occurs, there is no one making love to no one. How could this possibly be comprehensible to the mind?

The continued operation of all the functions in the state of freedom is an awesome way to live. It bears no resemblance to the stark emptiness that fear might paint it to be. People who tell me they don't want to give up the personal because they believe they would be giving up love or joy or deep feeling don't understand that the personal never existed. Nothing is given up. Love that appears to be personal is based on a mind-constructed sense of being separate. Love in this separate state involves a longing to merge with an other in order to be fulfilled. From the perspective of the vastness, the other does not exist. When the vastness sees everything out of itself to be made of itself, this is the ultimate intimacy. The moment-to-moment flavor of the vastness undulating within itself as it perceives itself through every particle of itself everywhere brings a love that is limitless, far surpassing anything the mind could construct as the ideal love it seeks.

Joy and pleasure are also awesome in their non-personal appearances. To live in the vastness of the naturally occurring state is to bathe in the ocean of non-personal pleasure and joy. This joy and pleasure, which belong to no one, are unlike any joy or pleasure that appear to refer or belong to a some-one. The emptiness is so full, so total, so infinitely blissful to itself.

These eyes see the incredible benevolence of the universe, which is completely trustworthy in all respects. There is nothing to fear. Everything in each moment is so well taken care of—and always has been. As the vastness peers out through these eyes onto the postmodern world, it feels moved to speak somehow to the myriad forms of suffering that are occurring.

Because the collision with emptiness occurred in my 28th year—without any search for it on my part, without a teacher or a traditional lineage, and before I had ever heard about no personal self—it seems that the vastness was training this circuitry to address the value of spiritual practices. The way the experience took place made it clear that the emptiness thrusts itself forward without waiting for any go-ahead from the mind. The infinite does not wait for the mind to grasp it in order for it to exist. In fact, realization of the infinite is outside the sphere of the mind. The infinite realizes itself out of itself.

This raises questions about the value of performing spiritual practices, studying ancient texts, or even living a "spiritual" life. Most practices imply the existence of a "me" who can do the practice and eventually accomplish a particular goal. But if a practice is undertaken by such a "me" in order to attain the non-locatable vastness of no personal self, then a conundrum or paradox presents itself: A personal doer is presumed to exist who must do the practices properly in order to achieve the realization that there is no personal doer.

But this reference to a personal doer runs totally counter to how the infinite exists. In this life, it has been clear ever since the experience at the bus stop that there never is, nor has there ever been, a personal doer anywhere. Prescribed techniques and lifestyles that insinuate an "I" who must "do" in order for awakening to occur presuppose a cause-and-effect relationship that simply does not exist. How can a personal "I" who doesn't exist be the one who must do something in order for awakening to occur?

Further, most spiritual practices presume that awakening is someplace else and must be reached or attained. But we are always the vastness—always! It is the naturally occurring human state. Where would the vastness go? Where could the infinite hide? What could we possibly need to do to become the vastness, when we already are it?

Many techniques also suggest that something must be eliminated, stopped, or purified in order for us to become who we really are. But the vastness is everything at all times. Nothing exists outside it, and nothing needs to be excluded from it. After all, we are talking about the infinite here.

In particular, there are spiritual traditions that imply that the mind must be stopped for the vastness to be realized. The assumption is that the relative activity of mind correlates with awakening. Of course, if a practice is undertaken to quiet or stop the mind, the result may be a quiet mind. But the infinite is not perceived through or grasped by the mind. The infinite realizes itself.

In this life, awakening did not occur because the mind stopped. No psychological or spiritual technique was involved, nor was there any locatable or apparent cause. Rather, the vastness showed itself in a mysterious manner—I was simply standing at a bus stop. How then can it be argued that some particular method or technique is required for awakening to occur?

Since I followed no prescribed techniques to realize the absence of the personal self, I cannot now encourage the practice of them. Strict practices may encourage the creation of more ideas about what the awakened state looks like as the mind attempts to figure out or approximate it. But how can the mind approximate what it cannot grasp? The vastness is unimaginable. Although it is always present, the mind cannot recognize it because the infinite is not perceived through the mind. The infinite perceives itself.

In no way, however, am I suggesting that practices should not be done, only that there is *no practitioner* who is the doer behind them. This is true of every activity: There is no walker, but walking occurs; no driver, but driving occurs; no thinker, but thinking occurs. Just because there is no practioner (and never has been) does not mean that practice will not take place. If it is obvious for a particular spiritual practice to occur, then it will. If it is obvious to meditate, chant, journey, circumambulate, travel, set up an altar, eat certain foods, perform certain acts, or visit certain teachers, these will be done, as things have always been done, by the mysterious, non-locatable doer that is behind everything. To base such practices on the idea that if they aren't done, you won't realize the vastness you already are—and will therefore be a spiritual failure—is to found your life on the successful functioning of some nonexistent "me."

The infinite reveals itself to the mind in mysterious, unimaginable, and ungraspable ways. But the mind, by its very nature, tends to reject what it cannot grasp. Thus, when it does encounter the vastness, it makes compelling attempts to devalue it. For example, many people have said to me, "I've experienced the vastness you're talking about, but it felt totally empty and flat. I'm not interested in going toward it again." What they're describing is not the ungraspable experiencing itself, but rather the mind contacting the ungraspable. When the mind sees experiences as being empty of the "someone-ness" it thought they were full of, it freaks out and begins to mount some convincing arguments for why the emptiness is totally undesirable.

In my case, the mind mounted an all-out effort to pathologize the emptiness of personal self in an attempt to get rid of it. This attempt proved unsuccessful. But many people have told me their minds were able to accomplish the task of making the emptiness appear to go away, only to be left with the memory of how unpleasant the contact with the ungraspable was for the mind. The mind then uses this memory as evidence that the emptiness must be avoided at all costs.

The contact of the mind with the emptiness of no personal reference point should never be taken to be the direct experience of the vastness, which in any case does not go through the mind. Rather, it is the experience of the mind's response to the vastness, and nothing more.

I have said before that there is no personal doer, but this should not be construed to mean that nothing gets done. In fact, there has never been a personal doer, yet it's obvious that the car gets driven, the children get fed, relationships get taken care of. As the mind sees things getting done, it concludes that there must be a someone who does them, otherwise doing would not occur. But the vastness has never waited for the mind to recognize that there is no doer for doing to occur. Doing has always occurred out of a placeless origin that is confounding to a mind that thrives on interpretation and insinuation. The vastness itself does not interpret doing to mean that there must be someone who does. It sees quite naturally that doing arises out of the same placeless origin as everything else.

⟞⟝

The vastness carries a non-personal desire to experience itself. This appears to be the purpose of human life—for the vastness to meet itself everywhere it turns. The notion of personal growth or inner development is contrary in every respect to the way the vastness exists. The quest to awaken implies a sense of futurity that precludes basking in what actually is right now. I am unable to see the value in any method of evolution that implies getting somewhere or becoming something different. As soon as one embarks on a path to somewhere, the awesomeness of what is, here and now, becomes unavailable. More important, the somewhere people are trying to arrive is actually not locatable, since it is everywhere all the time.

All ideas about accomplishing spiritual awakening are based on the assumption that there is a someone, a you, who can perform the practices and accomplish the goal. But this someone doesn't exist. Take, for example, the popular spiritual notion that we need to "get out of the way so the infinite can just flow through us." It is predicated on a nonexistent someone who can figure out how to surrender. We need to see that both spiritual and psychological practices, every single one of them, are based on taking ideas about who we are to be the truth of who we are. The idea that we are the doer behind our actions does not make us the doer, no matter how often we get hoodwinked into taking this idea to be truth.

Then there is the notion that we must stop the mind in order to be free. But who will stop the mind? Like everything else, the mind is just what it is. A mind that generates thoughts is not a problem; it is simply doing what minds do. The mind is made of the same vast emptiness as everything. Whether the mind is active or quiet, this emptiness never changes. Nor does the infinite wait for the mind to do or stop doing something in order for the vastness to reveal itself to itself. If the mind should stop, it simply does so as part of the unfathomable mystery.

A problem occurs only when the mind interprets the presence of thoughts to mean something—for example, that I'm bad or unspiritual and I'll never succeed in my meditation practice unless I stop the arising of thoughts. Thoughts and ideas are never a problem unless they are taken to be something they are not. If they are seen to be just thoughts and ideas, then they are not being identified with. Seeing things to be only and exactly what they are is the state of realization itself, because this is how the vastness always sees everything.

To see things for what they are is to see with the eyes of the vastness itself. This seeing is always occurring, whether or not we are consciously aware of it. Rather than getting caught by the mind, the vastness sees all the ways the mind attempts to hoodwink us into believing that we are an individual "I" who runs the show of life. It sees how the idea of who we are muscles its way into the front row of the mind and insists it is not just an idea, but who we really are. And it sees the infinite everywhere (where else could it be?) and then sees everyone searching for it.

The most common predicament people bring to me is the experience of feeling "cut off" from the infinite. They find this particularly painful if they have had clear experiences of the vastness which they then feel have "gone away." They want to know how they can stay in contact with the infinite at all times. This very question contains two implicit assumptions that pass themselves off as truth—that there is an "I" who is cut off from the infinite who could "apply itself" to reconnecting if it had the proper technique, and that the infinite has gone somewhere. These are prime examples of how ideas masquerade as truth.

In fact, there is no individual "I" who can figure out how to find the infinite again. More importantly, where would the infinite go? I mean, we aren't talking about something that could hide under the rug. If you could see things as only and exactly what they are, you would see that the "you" that is seeing is the vastness itself.

The "character work" prescribed by psychotherapy, as well as by some spiritual traditions, including Zen Buddhism, leads to a similar trap created by not seeing things to be simply what they are. A relaxation of being naturally arises if one is not seduced into taking ideas to be truth. This relaxation is antithetical to "character work," with its clear position about how we would be if our characters were worked on. When we knock on the door of "character work," we are invited into the labyrinth of futurity. It is inherently impossible to arrive at a goal that is predicated on an "I" that will get us there. Character work is based on the same erroneous belief that there is an individual doer who runs the show of life and can train itself to be a better "I."

Working as a psychologist has provided me with a front row seat in the theater of human suffering. It is apparent that traditional psychotherapy is founded on principles that pathologize human experience across the board and measure success according to how well we conform to definite ideas about what our human experience should look like. We are taught that we must "work through," "release," "deal with," "come to terms with," or "rid ourselves of" various aspects of our experience in order to live a satisfying life. We must "get in touch with our feelings," "find ourselves," "know what we want so we can get it," "not let anyone take advantage of us," and "find our true voice." Seen from the perspective of the vastness, all these ideas are just what they are—ideas. We should not mistake them for truth.

Over the years since the flowering of the springtime of the vastness, my work with psychotherapy clients has changed radically. In fact, I can no longer call what I do psychotherapy, since it in no way adheres to any standard principles of psychological theory or intervention. My goal for everyone is freedom—total freedom. I don't want them to change how they feel, work through childhood trauma, or get symptoms to stop. I want them to be free by seeing that things are just what they are.

I begin with everyone by asking them to tell me who they take themselves to be. This generally involves an in-depth exploration of all the ideas they have acquired from other people and have taken to be statements of truth about who they are. From early on, we're given a clear picture by our culture of the right somebody we're supposed to become, and most of us wholeheartedly undertake the enormous task of becoming that somebody.

Everyone I've worked with has become aware that they have constructed their "identities" out of information received by inference. They have inferred who they are from what other people have said to or about them and from the ways other people have treated them. Based on an interpretation of what all this information means about them, they have constructed who they take themselves to be. For example, Dad ignored me, therefore I must be unlovable or uninteresting. Or Mom always called me lazy, therefore it must be true.

These constructs exist in multiple spheres, not just in the mind. Personal reference points can be constructed in the emotional, physical, and energetic spheres as well. These multiple reference points for a sense of who we take ourselves to be can seem confusing at first, but all of them operate in a similar manner: They pass something off for what it's not. In the mind sphere, thoughts and ideas are passed off as who one really is. In the emotional sphere, it's feelings; in the physical sphere, sensations; in the energetic sphere, energetic vibrations or patterns.

The modern psychological world substantiates this deception when it encourages people to distinguish between the "true self" and the "false self," the true thoughts and the false thoughts, the true feelings and the false ones, the true and false sensations, even the true and false energetic frequencies. Who distinguishes between the true and the false? And true and false for whom? Thoughts, feelings, sensations, and energetic frequencies do not mean anything about some imaginary someone; they simply are what they are.

A further entanglement that occurs in the face of these ideas about who we are is that the negative is usually taken to be the truth. After all, the negative is so compelling and seems so deep. The positive is regarded as superficial and temporary but, ah, the negative! When it arises, we believe we're really in the presence of truth.

Connecting with others in our Western therapeutic culture is often based on a sharing of problems. When someone refuses to reveal what is most difficult in their lives, they are said to be "withholding" or "cut-off" or "untrustworthy." When their problems are known, however, they are thought to be revealing the truth about themselves.

This overvaluing of the negative is rampant in our culture. Just about every person who sits across from me in my office and speaks to me about their lives believes that what is negative about them is the most true. They are convinced that they carry something rotten at their core, that they are bad deep down, and that they will always return to the negative, which is the real bottom line. People have taken their worst fears to be the truth, and no one has pointed out to them that fears can only be what they are—fears.

The pathologizing of human experience, which has been perpetuated by the overpsychologizing of our culture, is another horror that has been masquerading as truth. We have been psychologized into believing that only certain experiences are appropriate. We have been given words that label our experience and thereby put us into an aversive relationship to it. The vastness is rigorously non-pathologizing because it is unable to perceive anything as wrong.

It is absurd to think that we have to get rid of certain aspects of our experience to be acceptable. As mentioned before, it would be like the ocean saying that it simply can not be the ocean as long as there is seaweed floating around in it. The ocean is the ocean, no matter what it contains. We are the vastness, and we contain everything—thoughts, emotions, sensations, preferences, fears, ideas, even identifications. Nothing has to go anywhere. In any case, where would it go?

Psychological directives that aim at a cure imply that certain thoughts or emotions are a sign we aren't acceptable. Spiritual directives that aim at a goal called realization or transcendence suggest that certain thoughts or emotions are impediments to spiritual unfolding. After all, they say, how can we be the vastness if we're experiencing confusion or fear, anger or sadness? But the presence of thoughts and feelings means only that thoughts and feelings are present. We interpret our experience to mean something (generally negative) about who we are. This interpretation creates suffering when it passes itself off for truth. But if it's seen to be what it is—an interpretation—it presents no problem; it's simply there too in the vastness.

Of course, we have to be careful not to use "seeing things for what they are" as a technique to get rid of emotions or mind-states that the mind deems undesirable. There is no experience whose presence is an indication that you are not the vastness. Therefore, there is no need to get rid of anything. Suffering is caused not by the presence of certain circumstances or experiences, but by the mind's interpretation of them.

After I speak to people about seeing things for what they are, they frequently go home and practice this "technique" rigorously, then conclude they have failed because what was seen didn't go away. But the vastness has no goal of ridding itself of anything. The vastness, which is what we really are, never suffers. Therefore, it never asks that anything be eliminated for suffering to cease.

The purpose of human life has been revealed. The vastness created these human circuitries in order to have an experience of itself out of itself that it couldn't have without them. Through this humanness, the substance we are all made of has an opportunity to love itself—and the love of the infinite for itself is awesome. The words "love," "bliss," and "ecstasy" only begin to describe the hugeness of the infinite's appreciation of itself that occurs through these circuitries.

We are all in this together. We are all made of the same infinite substance, and when a number of circuitries are consciously participating in the infinite simultaneously, there is a substantial increase in the volume of the love the infinite experiences for itself. This is the power of what has been called community. The wondrousness, the love, the ecstasy, the bliss of the infinite is constantly increasing as it surges within itself in a never-ending crescendo. There is no end to the vastness becoming vaster as it undulates within itself and amplifies the ecstatic love it has for itself out of itself.

This life is now lived in a state wherein the infinite is perceived as residing within an infinity. This is truly a non-experience that defies description, yet it seems to be how the infinite naturally shows itself to itself.

There is no end to all of this, just as there was no beginning. There are constant "bus hits," as I now call them, in which the infinite expands yet again and again. The substance of the vastness is so directly perceivable to itself in every moment that the circuitry at times requires another adjustment phase to get used to more infinite awareness. When asked who I am, the only answer possible is: I am the infinite, the vastness that is the substance of all things. I am no one and everyone, nothing and everything—just as you are.

EPILOGUE

CONVERSATIONS WITH THE VASTNESS

Since there is nothing to meditate on,
there is no meditation.
Since there is nowhere to go astray,
there is no going astray.
Although there is an innumerable variety
of profound practices,
they do not exist for your mind in its true state.
Since there are no two such things as
practice and practitioner,
if, by those who practice or do not practice,
the practitioner of practice is seen to not exist,
thereupon the goal of practice is reached
and also the end of practice itself.
—Padmasambhava

Q: You say you can't really recommend any practices because there is no doer to do them. What about those of us who have not had bus stop experiences like you have? What do we do in the meantime?

A: Whatever is being done by the non-locatable doer that has always been the doer. There isn't a you who has to decide what needs to be done in order for doing to happen. I'm not saying there are no spiritual practices. There is just no practitioner. When practices are based on getting a someone to do the practice properly so the right result will be achieved, they sustain and even amplify the belief in a separate, individual self.

The non-locatable doer that's behind everything shows itself in obvious ways. If it's obvious to meditate, you'll be meditating. If it's obvious to be politically active, you'll be politically active. There's not a someone who has to do your life in a particular way for it to be worthwhile or valuable. There is no one to whom any of it refers—thoughts, feelings, actions, events. It just is what it is and always has been. It's truly awesome.

We experience this awe when we look at nature—at trees or flowers or mountains or oceans. "Aren't they incredible?" we say. It seems easy to see there is no locatable doer behind nature; there is not a someone to whom it refers. Yet people tend to feel that they are separate from the natural sphere. They recognize that nature is awesome in its mysteriousness, but they take their own lives to be about a someone who is responsible for making things happen. If certain things are occurring, it's interpreted to mean something about this illusory someone, and if other things are occurring, it means something else. Then they go into therapy to try to change themselves—to make themselves into a better someone so they can have a better life.

But to this circuitry it's perfectly clear that everyone and everything *is* the vastness. When another circuitry presents a constructed "I-ness" and tries to pass it off as who they are, it is immediately seen for what it is—a bunch of ideas or feelings or body sensations. It's a construct that is just there too, like everything else.

Behind most spiritual practices is the belief that you have to get someplace you're not—a destination called realization or enlightenment. But realization isn't someplace else; it's the naturally occurring human state. It doesn't belong to anybody. It's who we all are. Spiritual practices also set up many pictures of what this state looks like. For example, when I described how much fear was present, people told me the fear meant that something must be wrong, because fear was an indication that I wasn't in the proper state. But fear is just what it is, and it's there too in the vastness of who we are.

Q: What about the experience of choosing one action or direction over another?

A: The moment-to-moment experience here is that it's a choiceless life because there is no one choosing. Actions are never preceded by thoughts or feelings or by any attempt to figure things out. Everything is very immediate. Choicelessness is the experience of the obvious in a moment-to-moment way.

Of course, in most lives there is the sense that there is a "me" making choices and that, based on these choices, particular actions occur. There are ideas about who is choosing and ideas about what constitutes the right choice as opposed to the wrong one. These ideas set up what I call the sphere of the constructed reference point. When the eyes of this reference point are being seen through rather than the eyes of the vastness, it looks to the mind like only a very limited range of actions is available, when in fact the possibilities are limitless. The mind then appropriates the action and says, "I did it," and the action appears to relate to a someone behind it. But this never changes the fact that there is never a personal doer behind anything. Because the process is so infinite and ungraspable, the mind creates the notion of choice in an attempt to understand it.

Q: Given what you just said, could you comment on the fact that you offer these talks?

A: There are a lot of pictures about what this naturally occurring state looks like. This life seems to have been trained by the vastness not to match any of those pictures. I mean, I was standing at a bus stop, for goodness sakes! How can you say what I was doing that caused the experience to happen? This life is just a describer, and one of the things it sees is that this state does not belong to anyone. It's not something you can get from someone. It's who everyone is. From here, the highest volume is the sound of the infinite ocean that we all are.

Q: Since this isn't something that can be grasped by the mind, it's been said that certain teachers who live in this state can transmit it to others. Of course, you didn't receive this from a living teacher. But do you think it's possible for one person to transmit it to another?

A: The idea of transmission suggests that it belongs to somebody and can be given to somebody else. But that is not at all how the vastness perceives itself out of itself. It is who everyone already is. How could it be transmitted? All this circuitry can perceive is the vastness that everything is made of. When other circuitries are related to only as the vastness, it may tend to bring the vastness foreground in their experience.

Q: Is the vastness you are referring to perceived as love and light?

A: The mind has to know that it can't grasp what I'm about to describe. The vastness is perceiving itself out of itself at every moment within every particle of itself everywhere simultaneously. This is what I call the sense organ of the infinite. It doesn't have a flavor to it; it is simply perceiving itself.

At the bus stop this circuitry was thrust into consciously participating in the sense organ of the vastness which is perceiving itself out of itself all the time. The moment the circuitry begins to consciously participate, the vastness has a particular flavor. I can't describe it in personal terms because everything I see now is only apparently personal. Instead of light or love, I would use the term undulation—the undulation of the vastness. For example, if you are sitting in a hot bath and don't move, you don't feel the heat of the water. As soon as you move, the heat is felt. In the same way, the human circuitry gives the vastness the possibility of experiencing its own vastness through what I call the undulation.

The mind can't grasp this. But who you are is always grasping itself all the time. There's no one that has to start grasping for it to be grasping itself. It is occurring simultaneously with everything that is taken to be who you are. If you want to call it love, I'll agree, but I wouldn't want it to be mistaken for the love that refers to a personal self.

The vastness definitely experiences pleasure in experiencing itself. As a matter of fact, this pleasure seems to be the purpose of human life—to have the human circuitry consciously participate in the sense organ of the vastness that it is made of. After all, it is who we all are. It's hard to give a visual description because it lies outside the sphere of perception. What I can say is that every form that is ordinarily taken to be full of something—particular importance or meaning to a particular reference point, for example—is seen to be empty. It's like a line drawn in the sand. The line as well as what is inside and outside of it are all made of the same sand.

Q: Is there anything I can do to accelerate this happening in my case? Or is it just grace?

A: There is no one I could instruct to do something to make you the vastness. That's already and always who you are. The instruction to perform certain practices is predicated on a reference point, but to the vastness this reference point simply doesn't exist. The question of who can do what to get to where you already are seems absurd.

As to whether it happens by grace, I don't know. I was just standing at a bus stop. There's an incredible mysteriousness about all of this. There wasn't a someone who was trying to trust or accept or surrender the best she could in order for this to happen. I didn't even want it. So I can't tell you what to do because that would be referring to a someone who is taken to be the doer. That which is the non-locatable doer is taking care of everything all the time in such infinitely mysterious ways.

Look at this world. What if trees or clouds or planets or stars waited for the mind to figure them out in order for them to exist? Or imagine if the body waited for the mind to figure out how to grow a baby before it became pregnant. "How do I make this brain? Where do I put this heart? Maybe I should get the blood moving now." This is all taken care of by that which lies so completely outside of the mind's ability to perceive it that trust isn't even an issue.

That's why I give only two suggestions. The first is to see things to be just what they are, because that is how the vastness is always seeing things. Thoughts are thoughts. Emotions are emotions. The body is just the body. It's the mind's interpretation of things that ends up creating suffering—the sense that there is a problem, that fear or anger or sadness means there's something wrong with me, that certain emotions or experiences have to be eliminated for me to be OK, that something needs to be practiced or achieved in order to become the infinite. The mind is constantly interpreting in this way, while the vastness just looks around and sees that things are just what they are.

The second suggestion, which is actually a non-suggestion, is to follow the obvious, because that is how the mysterious doer behind everyone's life is constantly revealing the truth of each moment Now I'm not saying you need to figure out what the obvious is and then follow it. The mind doesn't usually perceive the obvious, and it tends to devalue what it can't perceive. Take the expression "it's just too obvious," for example. It's not complicated or painful enough. The mind is drawn to complexity and struggle. That's the sphere of the mind.

Q: When you do what seems like the obvious, how do you know your mind isn't subtly deceiving you to make you think you're doing the obvious when in fact you're not?

A: What you're describing is the mind constructing a reference point that then scans with its own standards for the true obvious. "How do I know I'm following the obvious? Is this really the obvious or is it a false obvious? When I find the true obvious, I'll go with that." But the obvious is not identified by the mind. And the vastness that we all are is actually seeing the mind to be exactly what it is, doing exactly what minds do.

Q: I'm not aware of scanning. I feel compelled to do what my intuition tells me is obvious, and in the moment it feels very natural and graceful. But I know I'm being manipulated.

A: You are describing how the mind tends to be looked to as the perceiver of truth. But the obvious doesn't wait for the mind to perceive it for the obvious to be lived. Now the mind doesn't like to be bypassed, so it raises doubts about whether the obvious was the right action or the wrong one. Was it the obvious, or was I hoodwinked? That's just the mind responding the way it does to what it cannot grasp. The vastness doesn't require that the mind be different. It just sees it for what it is. It's not a problem. It's only when the doubts the mind raises are taken for the truth—or for some problem or issue that has to be resolved before you can really know what's obvious—that suffering occurs.

Q: Aren't you just talking about a vaster, more universal mind here? I don't think the mind should be disregarded.

A: The mind has to be seen for what it is. It's made of the same substance as the infinite, just like everything else. To say that the vastness is infinite mind is really no different than saying it is infinite body or infinite emotions. Why say infinite mind? Why not just say it is the infinite, which sees the mind to be what it is?

I'm certainly not suggesting that you devalue the mind. The vastness doesn't see the mind as a problem, as a sign that there is something wrong that needs to be changed in some way. The mind is there too, and it's made of the same substance. In the West it's important to see the mind for what it is, because the Western mind has been trained to take the driver's seat, to construct and hold the reference point.

Q: What drew you to become a psychotherapist after having this experience?

A: One of the missions of the vastness through this circuitry seems to be to reach psychotherapists. I have started training groups for therapists because I want this to be conveyed to those who are in the business of trying to help end suffering. There are so many rigid ideas about how we are supposed to be and what is considered healthy and unhealthy. Instead of supporting people in seeing things to be what they are, the profession has compiled a diagnostic manual that pathologizes a broad range of human experience. Everything that arises is interpreted to have some psychological meaning, and certain things are considered undesirable—abnormal, dysfunctional—and in need of being eliminated for "healing" or "cure" to occur. But who is going to get rid of them, and why would they? The infinite doesn't ask anything to be eliminated. The presence of any thought, feeling, or behavior does not for a minute affect the infinity of the infinite.

Q: What about suffering? Is there unnecessary suffering, or is suffering just perfect, like everything else?

A: Suffering occurs when something is taken for what it's not, rather than for what it is. Taking the negative reference point, the negative self-image, to be the truth is rampant in the West. The negative seems so much truer and deeper than anything else. When people share their problems, they feel like they really know one another. The glorification of the negative is incredibly powerful.

If the negative ideas or beliefs or feelings are simply seen for what they are, there is no suffering. But when they are taken to be who I am, there is the sense that something must be terribly wrong with me and unless I change and rid myself of this negativity, my life isn't going to be acceptable. This is what I call the case for the prosecution: the negative reference points are constructed and then are used to generate all this evidence for why they are really the truth.

People say to me, "Of course this is who I am.

Look at how I behave and feel and think. Clearly there's something wrong with me." They may even point to therapists they have seen or books they have read to support their case. "You see! I don't act the way this author says you're supposed to or the way my former therapist told me was healthy or spiritual."

In aikido, you are taught that when your opponent attacks you, you actually use his momentum to set him off balance. If you try to resist him, you create unnecessary conflict. It's the same with all the thoughts and feelings and other experiences that arise in the ocean of ourselves. The ocean never resists them; it never creates a negative reference point, saying, "Damn, that seaweed is still there. There must be something terribly wrong with me." When they arise, the ocean just sees them for what they are, and they pass away naturally.

These questions and answers were excerpted from public talks given in the spring of 1996.

Acknowledgments

Acknowledgment follows for those who have had their part in the mysterious functioning of the infinite as it has manifested in this life. There are many who have shown themselves to be significant in their participation in bringing forth the description you have just read.

·

Lisa and Myron Segal, my parents, for bringing this life into the world. Daniel and Robert Segal, my brothers, for being co-participants in the life of family. Maharishi Mahesh Yogi, for describing the transcendent field. The Parisian mass transit system, for providing a bus stop in lieu of a bodhi tree. All the psychotherapists who were unsuccessful in their efforts to cure the vastness. Steven Kruszynski, for being a companion in the wintertime and a father for Arielle.

·

All those who provided recognition of the presence of the vastness in the winter of its expression: Jean Klein, Jack Kornfield, Christopher Titmuss, Andrew Cohen, Gangaji, Hameed Ali, Reb Anderson, Poonjaji, Ram Dass, John Tarrant.

Ramana Maharshi, present in the change of seasons.

•

With the emerging of the springtime, the following have shown themselves to be playmates in the vastness: Stephan Bodian, for bringing the vastness out of the closet and for being a talented editor and friend; Michael Batliner, for his radical enthusiasm; those in the first wave who came and then shared with a larger community what they recognized: Richard Miller, John Prendergast, Judith Shiner, Elliott Isenberg, Peter Scarsdale, Lela Landman, Krishna. Neil Lupa, for his camaraderie in the vastness. And all those who have participated in the description of the vastness in discussions, private sessions, and small groups.

•

To Arielle, who was born into the infinite.

Sources

Padmasambhava poem, p. 157 © 1975 Francesca Fremantle
and Chogyam Trungpa, from *The Tibetan Book of the Dead*,
translated by Francesca Fremantle and Chogyam Trungpa,
Shambala Publications, 1975

Rainer Maria Rilke poem, p. 1, © 1991 Stephen Mitchell (translator), from *The Enlightened Mind*, Harper Collins, 1991

Rainer Maria Rilke poem, p. 85, © 1982 Stephen Mitchell
(translator) from *Selected Poetry of Rainer Maria Rilke*, Ran-
dom House, 1982

Rumi poems, pp. 11, 45, 137 © Coleman Barks, by Rumi, translated into English by John Moyne and Coleman Barks and
contained in *Open Secret*, Threshold Books, 1984

Rumi poem, p. 73 © Coleman Barks, by Rumi, translated into
English by John Moyne and Coleman Barks and contained in
Unseen Rain, Threshold Books, 1986

Theodore Roethke poem, p. 35 (from "Journey to the Interior"),
© Theodore Roethke from *The Collected Poems of Theodore
Roethke*, Anchor/Doubleday, 1974

Wallace Stevens poem, p. 107 (from "The Snowman"), © 1923,
renewed 1951 by Wallace Stevens, from *The Collected Poems
of Wallace Stevens*, Alfred A. Knopf, 1951